Financial Literacy: How to Gain Financial Intelligence, Financial Peace and Financial Independence

A Guide to Personal Finance in Your Twenties and Thirties

Shaun M. Durrant

contained within this document, including, but not limited to, errors, omissions, or inaccuracies.

Table of Contents

INTRODUCTION 1

WHY FINANCIAL LITERACY MATTERS 2

Who am I? 4

CHAPTER 1: GETTING OUT OF DEBT WHEN YOU DON'T MAKE ENOUGH 7

THE MILLENNIAL WORLD 8

Mistake #1 - Minimum Payments 11

Mistake #2 - Being Overly Reliant on Credit Cards 13

Mistake #3 - Disorganized Payments 14

Mistake #4 - Unrealistic Living Standards 15

HABITS THAT YOU NEED 16

Habit #1 - Retirement Planning 17

Habit #2 - Budgeting 18

Habit #3 - Set Goals 20

Habit #4 - Managing Money 21

Habit #5 - Flexibility and Growth 22

TIPS FOR GETTING OUT OF DEBT IN YOUR 20S AND 30S 23

Prioritize Fiscal Discipline 23

Consolidate Your Debt 24

Pay Intelligently 24

Develop a Side Gig 25

Reduce Expenses 25

Build an Emergency Fund 26

Seek Help 27

Understand Your Credit Score 27

CHAPTER 2: REDUCING MONTHLY EXPENSES 29

BUDGETING 101 30

Minimalist Budget 31

Emergency Fund Contribution 33

Goal Related Contributions 35

Long Term Savings Contribution 35

Side Hustle and Self Improvement Contribution 36

Charity 37

Using Apps 37

REDUCING EXPENSES 38

Set Realistic Goals 39

Rely on Yourself 40

Use Tools 41

Cover the Essentials..41

Wants and Needs 42

Limit Media Consumption 43

Entertain Intelligently..44

View the Long Term 45

Cash Cleanse 46

Shop Smarter 46

Buy Used 48

CHAPTER 3: BUILDING WEALTH - WAYS TO START EARNING MORE 51

MONETIZE EXISTING RESOURCES...52

Building Income Streams - Preliminary Work 55

THE BEST WAYS TO BUILD WEALTH...59

Microinvesting Apps 59

Search for a Better Job 60

Ask for a Raise 61

Freelancing 62

Online Businesses 65

Selling Courses 67

Etsy 68

Local Gigs...68

eBay Selling 69

Real Estate Investing 69

Daytrading, Cryptotrading, Forex Trading 71

CHAPTER 4: FUNDING YOUR GOALS AND DREAMS.................................... 73

DEFINING YOUR GOALS...75

Invert 76

Creating a Roadmap..78

HOW TO FUND YOUR DREAMS 81

Get Out of Debt First...81

Research and Reverse Engineer..82

Timelines...83

Discipline 84

Scale Well 84

Save Wisely..86

High Yield Savings...87

One Time Windfalls 87

Automate...88

Plan...88

Be Prepared 90

CHAPTER 5: TAKING YOUR FIRST STEPS TO SAVE CASH 91

GETTING STARTED WITH RETIREMENT 92
   Calculate 93
   Understand Compounding 94
   Fix a Goal 96
   Use Retirement Accounts 97
   Build an Emergency Fund 99
   Keep it Liquid 100
HABITS THAT BOOST SAVING 101
   Consistency 101
   Don't Wait 102
   Talk it Out 104
   Keep Cash in an Account 104

CHAPTER 6: HOW TO INVEST IN YOUR 20S AND 30S 107

OPPORTUNITIES 110
   Certificates of Deposit 110
   Stocks 111
   Bonds 112
   Funds 115
   Real Estate Investment Trusts 118
   Other Instruments 119
   Real Estate 120
TIPS FOR SENSIBLE INVESTMENT 123
   Know Your Risk Profile 123
   Diversify 124
   Educate 125
   Minimize Fees 126
   Start Slow 127
   Ask for Advice 128
   Remain as Objective as Possible 129
A FINAL WORD 130

CHAPTER 7: MANAGING MONEY AS A COUPLE 131

WHEN SHOULD YOU TALK ABOUT IT? 132
   Blueprints 134
MONEY MANAGEMENT TIPS 137
   Discuss Prenuptial or Postnuptial Agreements 137
   Be Honest 138
   Develop Goals 139
   Bank Accounts 139
   Share Tasks 141
   Plan to Attack Debt 141

HANDLING ARGUMENTS AND DISAGREEMENTS 143

Empathize...143

Enforce Boundaries..144

Compromise...144

Talk About Money 145

Seek Help 146

CHAPTER 8: THE PSYCHOLOGY OF WEALTH 147

THE WEALTH MINDSET 148

Think for the Long Term 149

Read and Learn..150

Spend Money to Make Money...151

Persistence...153

Work Smart 153

Keep Good Company 154

Seek a Mentor 155

Expand..155

Understand Risk...156

Eliminate Scarcity Thinking...157

CONCLUSION 159

REFERENCES 161

Introduction

"It's not how much money you make, but how much money you keep, how hard it works for you, and how many generations you keep it for." ~ *Robert Kiyosaki*

Meet Bob. He's just graduated with a degree that he's worked hard to achieve in four years. He's looking forward to entering the adult world (that is, the real world, not the make believe world of college) and start investing. There's just one problem: Bob owes $26,900 in student loan debt. If he had attended a private school, he'd probably owe close to $35,000 in debt (Hess, 2019).

"That's not a lot" you might be thinking. If Bob earns a salary of $50,000 at his job (assuming he has one lined up), it's around half of his first year's pay. If you're thinking this, then you're in the right place. You're exactly the kind of person who needs this book!

America and the rest of the world might be experiencing a pandemic right now, but over the last two decades another disease has been spreading. This disease is ignorance. Specifically, ignorance of financial matters and of simple personal finance knowledge.

It isn't the fault of the average American. We attend schools and universities and fill our heads with all kinds of useful information such as the average GDP of Argentina in the 1980s, but we cannot balance a checkbook if our life depended on it. We look at numbers and financial jargon and run away screaming.

As a result, we end up making less than intelligent decisions with our money. The real world throws enough problems at a person. There's no need to compound them by inventing ones of your own! Managing your money and directing it towards the right resources is a fundamental skill that everyone ought to have.

This is what you're going to learn in this book. Unfortunately, the current education system deems everything you're about to learn as being unnecessary. No one knows what the reason for this is. Perhaps the previous generation didn't need to worry about such things.

However, the world we're living in today makes this knowledge imperative. After all, we're not dealing with the safe and stable world that our parents lived in.

Why Financial Literacy Matters

Everyone knows that they need to have some level of financial knowledge. After all, you need money to pay for the things that you want in your life. You'll need to figure out how you'll pay for them as well. So far so good. The problem is that most people don't take into account the variety of factors that can affect the money they earn, or their cash inflow.

Take Bob's case for example. Sure, his student loan debt is slightly more than half his annual salary. However, this assumes he doesn't pay taxes. Next, he needs to pay for his living expenses. If he lives in most American cities, he'll need to buy a car. Being fresh out of college, he's likely not going to have money to buy one in cash so that means he'll need to draw another loan to pay for it.

Then there's health insurance. His old college insurance plan won't cover him anymore. He paid a few hundred dollars to insure himself through the old plan, but he will now need to pay a lot more for an individual plan (dental insurance is extra, as he'll soon find out). He needs to find a place to live, which will involve a credit score check.

Given the loans he has on his record, his score isn't going to be very high. This means he'll pay more in rent than the average person or will have to live in a less desirable neighborhood. This increases the maintenance costs he'll have to pay for his car and his place of abode.

All of these expenses take a toll. Since we're assuming Bob is the average American college graduate, he'll likely take 20 years to pay his student loan off (Carter, 2019). He'll be a middle aged man by the time he's debt free.

Being the average American and having very little financial savvy, he's unlikely to be debt free because he'll probably have assumed a mortgage by then and have ensured he'll be a servant to his debt till the age of 70. Not a pretty picture is it?

This is what awaits most American today and it's astonishing that no one thinks this is a problem. You've taken the right step in reading this book. If you're someone who wishes to escape this abysmal fate, then you're in the right place. I'm not going to give you the same old advice of "always make a budget!"

Well, actually that is one of the things I'll be telling you. However, you're smart enough to understand that there's more to money management than just that. It's when people think beyond their personal budgets (even if they don't have one) that intimidation sets in.

They look at the stock market, real estate market, certificates of deposit, bonds, savings accounts, side gigs, and startup hustles and think there's no way they'll ever achieve any of that. Let's run a little thought experiment.

Let's say I could correctly calculate how much food you eat in a month and managed to gather all of it together in one place. I then bring you to this place and show you the mountain of food in front of you. Would you be able to eat all of it at once? Would you even think you'd be able to eat that much food in a month?

Probably not! Approaching personal finance is pretty much the same. You need to take things step by step. This book addresses multiple topics in the personal finance space, right from the very basics of getting debt free when you're not making enough money, to the more advanced topic of investing intelligently when you're in your 20s and 30s.

I'll also help you figure out what your monetary psychological profile is in the final chapter. How you think about money impacts your life. Taking the time to figure this out will pay you rich dividends.

The only question at this juncture is: Why should you listen to me?

Who am I?

It says Shaun M. Durrant on the cover so you already know that's my name. I'm probably older than you thanks to being in my 40s. I'm someone who has struggled through the situations I mentioned earlier. Our friend Bob isn't completely fictional. There's a lot of my life situation embedded in his example.

I struggled with student loan debt and low income right out of college. I was lucky enough to graduate into an economy that was still booming and didn't have financial crashes every decade or so. Through hard work and intense self education, I managed to rid myself of my debt and build my wealth.

Throughout all of this, there wasn't anyone who held my hand and guided me through all the important decisions. I had to figure things out by myself and I took a few blows here and there. However, I'm thankful for these setbacks because they taught me more about money than anything else in my life.

It's easy to tell someone to do this or that, but I'm keenly aware of the current struggles that young people face in this country. It's scary to think of how little support there is for people who wish to rid themselves of debt. Sure, there are debt relief programs, but these are a bit like applying a band aid on a broken limb.

It's much better to avoid getting into the problematic situation in the first place. This is my intent when writing this book. I'm appalled at the lack of financial education in this country and the attitude that the education system adopts. The young people of America have to sit through hours and hours of general education courses covering different languages and cultures, but they aren't taught anything about what's truly in their wallet.

As someone who's passionate about all things money, my aim is to rectify this situation as much as possible. The more people who read this book, the better off we'll all be. I genuinely believe that, so thank you for buying this book. You're doing yourself and your future generations a huge favor.

Not only are you working to rid yourself of your debt burden, you're allowing yourself to educate your kids and their kids by helping them make the right decisions. This is how wisdom spreads, and you deserve a pat on the back for taking the right first step.

It's time to take a further step. Are you ready to get rid of the debt that plagues you? Let's go.

Chapter 1:

Getting out of Debt When You

Don't Make Enough

You've just read what the statistics say about average student loan debt. Well, it gets much worse than just student debt. The average American graduating college does so with debt. They're in the red before they've earned a single penny. It's a lot like attempting to win a race by starting well behind your competition.

This is why people these days feel as if they're on a hamster wheel. The faster they run, the more firmly they stay in place. Debt is the reason for this. You cannot hope to grow your wealth until you get rid of your debt. Not enough people understand how critical this is. They go ahead and assume more debt such as car loans and mortgages telling themselves they're paying for "necessary" things.

The only thing that is necessary is for you to get rid of your debt. That should be your utmost priority if you're carrying any. It doesn't matter what kind of debt you're carrying. It could be student loans, car loans, credit card loans, and so on. A mortgage that doesn't create cash flow from the property is also a debt. The old adage of "paying yourself" by avoiding rental payments is nonsense.

You cannot practically get rid of a mortgage, but you should work to develop more income streams from it as quickly as you can. This means you set up another source of cash that can reduce your mortgage burden or you find a way to make your property generate cash flow. I'll talk about how to do this in later chapters.

At this point, it's important for you to understand the world you're living in. Why would you need to know this? You're smart and can see what's happening around you. My reasoning behind exploring this topic is to get you to see how critical it is for you to manage your money intelligently and why your ignorance could end up costing you much more than what you bargained for.

The Millennial World

Millennials have received a lot of criticism from sections of the media for being lazy or for complaining too much. Without getting into the politics of this, such criticism is unfair to say the least. The world that exists today is quite different from what it was a generation or two ago.

Back in the 90s, America was unashamedly optimistic. The Soviet Union had just fallen and left this country as the world's sole superpower. There was no competition to worry about. Even Japan, which had been rising economically, had fallen into a recession that continues to this day.

The stock market was booming. Any wars that began ended swiftly and conclusively in favor of America. It was in this world that most millennials were born and naturally, they came to expect things to be a certain way. Then the millennium dawned and right on cue, the stock markets collapsed.

Just as the market recovered, one of the biggest financial scandals involving the energy trading company Enron erupted. As everyone was coming to grips with Enron, the September 11th terrorist attacks happened. This started an endless cycle of wars that America is involved in to this day. At least the housing market was fine. That bubble burst in 2008. The period from 2007 to 2009 was one of the most harrowing economic crises that this country has gone through.

While the stock market recovered and pushed higher, it was clear that the economic recovery was just on paper. Wealth was being concentrated in the hands of a few and opportunity wasn't equally available anymore. A Stanford dropout could raise billions on a harebrained idea thanks to connections but someone without the same brand value was left out in the cold.

Over the past decade, the economic system has seemed to improve but has actually become more unstable. The tiniest shove could send things toppling. Many thought the rise of China would be the catalyst. Instead, it was the Covid-19 pandemic that brought the economy to its knees.

Millennials (and Gen-Xers) who were told to work hard in college and secure good jobs now find themselves financially uneducated and loaded with debt without a salary to pay those debts down. Imagine working for a company for close to a decade and finding yourself out in the cold.

This is the world that faces you if you're about to graduate or have recently graduated. The world is unstable and tying yourself to a single source of income puts you one step removed from poverty. You cannot rely on your job to be there at all times. Multiple streams of income and zero debt aren't a luxury anymore; they're a necessity.

Creating this situation might seem intimidating but that's why you're here. It's natural and perfectly fine to wonder how you're going to achieve all of this. This is why it's important for you to take things step by step. Do a little bit everyday and you'll reap the rewards of consistency.

I've walked you through this painful picture to help you realize that the stability you think you have in your life is an illusion. As long as debt remains in the picture, you're precariously close to the edge. It won't take much to send you into freefall. While losing your job or source of income hurts, you can deal with that situation a lot better if you have zero debt.

You need to make eliminating debt a top priority in your life. This means you need to cut down on every other expense until your debt is paid off. You need to be ruthless with it. Would you allow a pest or a rodent to live in your home without permission? Would you allow sickness to consume you endlessly? You wouldn't.

If these situations happened, you would take steps to remedy them as soon as possible. You'd handle them before you even thought of doing anything else. Adopt this attitude with your debt. You'll realize how much of a burden you're carrying once you get rid of it. Debt puts the brakes on your money goals and you won't go anywhere with it.

Often, our habits drive us deeper into debt or keep us firmly rooted in it. Let's take a look at some of the things that do you no favors. Don't despair if you spot some of these habits within yourself. Becoming aware of your habits is the first step in your journey to rectifying the situation. In fact, awareness is a huge part of the solution.

Mistake #1 - Minimum Payments

This mistake applies mostly to credit card or auto debts. It arises from a lack of awareness of what debt is and how repayments work. Every loan you draw has two components within it. There's the principal and then there's the interest. Interest is what the lender charges you for the privilege of borrowing money from them.

This is the profit that the lender makes by giving you money. For example, if you draw a loan on a car that costs $20,000 at five percent interest over 48 months, your monthly payment will be $461 per month. Over the course of 48 months, you'll pay $22,128 for a car that costs $20,000. This represents an additional amount of $2,128 or 10.6% that you'll be paying. Even worse, the car you've bought will decrease in value. So what you're doing is paying $22,128 for a car that will probably be worth $10,000 by the time you're done making payments.

In short, you'll have paid $22,128 for a car that's worth $10,000. No one who does this can get rich. It's just common sense. How can you make money when you're paying two dollars for something that costs a dollar?

The monthly payment of $461 includes both the principal and interest component. Some loans are interest only and you'll have to make separate payments in order to pay the principal. As long as you're paying just interest, the principal that you borrowed remains firmly in place.

This means your payments are not reducing your debt. The money you borrowed continues to exist and will exist in perpetuity unless you take action to pay it off. Lots of people fall into this trap with credit card debt. They make the minimum payment to avoid defaults and penalties. However, their balances keep getting carried over.

Meanwhile, they make new purchases with the card every month, which causes the amount they're borrowing to keep growing.

Mistake #2 - Being Overly Reliant on Credit Cards

Credit cards are great things. In the right hands, they have the power to bring you more free stuff than you can ever imagine. However, in the wrong hands they can ruin the person using them. Credit card companies are well aware of this and highlight the positives to draw people in.

Some companies and banks are unscrupulous enough to sign customers up for credit cards they don't need or want. The financial system is also rigged to make us slaves to credit card debt. Did you know that if you have no credit cards to your name or no debt to your name, your credit score will be lower than someone who is carrying debt (El Issa & O'Shea, 2020)?

We live in a system that punishes people for good financial behavior. Is it any wonder that so many people don't have a clue about how to manage their money? Coming back to credit cards, it's a good idea to have one that gives you free stuff. Spend a small amount of money on it every week, less than $100, so that your credit score is in decent shape.

The exception is if you're carrying student loan debt. In that case, you have no business carrying a credit card. If you have one right now and are carrying student loans, take a pair of scissors and chop up your credit card right now. When the card expires, notify your bank that you don't need it anymore and cancel the account.

Spend only what you can afford. Credit cards kick the payments due down the road, but it's a lot like pushing dirt under the carpet. At some point, it's going to stink and you'll have a huge problem on your hands. You can also imagine it as digging a hole and piling dirt in front of you.

Don't utilize more than 10% of your credit limit on a single card or over 30% of your overall credit limit. Pay off your balances in full to avoid falling into the minimum payment trap.

Building up credit card debt drills yourself into a hole that can be impossible to climb out of. Watch how much you spend on credit cards. Leave them at home if you're unable to control your impulses.

Mistake #3 - Disorganized Payments

A singular characteristic of people who struggle with debt is their inability to organize their payment schedules. Such people typically have multiple payments they need to make every month. In the whirl of trying to organize the cash to pay for everything, they forget some payments or end up paying just the minimum amounts.

If this applies to you, don't worry. The first thing to do is to consolidate all of these payments into a single or a couple manageable ones. Speak to a debt resolution advisor if needed. It's important that you prioritize debt payment as much as possible. You should not hesitate to seek help to make your debt payments easier.

Late payments make a bad situation worse. Late fees will combine with your interest to make paying your debts much more difficult. Collect enough of these late fees and soon you'll be paying interest on them as well. The hamster wheel starts spinning faster and you'll need to run at full speed to merely remain in place.

No person can function at a high level with such constraints in place. This situation is easily avoided once you make the decision to rid yourself of your debt. Look at all the things it's robbing you off and resolve to get rid of it as quickly as possible.

Mistake #4 - Unrealistic Living Standards

We live in a world where something is constantly being sold to us. Advertising methods have become so sophisticated that the moments when someone isn't selling us anything seem odd. We feel compelled to buy things we don't need to prove points to people we don't know.

Social media is full of people faking their lives in a bid to gain more attention. While there is a case to be made for making money through such means, the large majority of people do it solely for the attention. This puts them right in the spending trap, which is where advertisers want them all along.

The rise of businesses that allow you to rent fancy clothes indicates how ridiculous the situation is. People rent clothes and fancy accessories from such places in order to post selfies and present a lifestyle that isn't grounded in reality. We think we're entitled to the finest things and don't spend too much time trying to figure out whether such things really bring happiness.

All that matters is that the influencer on Instagram posted a picture at a certain exotic location. This means we need to do the same. None of this does our wallet any favors. Debt can seem unreal in the face of social validation. In the age before social media, we used to refer to this as succumbing to peer pressure. The rise of digital media outlets has only made the problem worse.

Take a step back and ask yourself how important such validation really is. Do you need to assume a high cost phone plan just so that you can hold an overrated iPhone in your hands? I'm not saying you need to deprive yourself of the good things in life. It's just that the things that make you feel good often don't need massive expenditure.

This is what advertisers are trying to divert you from. They try their best to convince you that you need to buy fancy clothes and have a fancy car or else that guy/girl won't look at you twice. They sell you expensive jewelry with the implicit promise that you'll attract more attention and validation.

Social media charms you by providing shots of dopamine. Dopamine is a hormone that is secreted when you feel good. The validation of our peers results in a shot of dopamine to our system that is comparable to a snort of cocaine (Haynes, 2018).

No one in their right mind would rush out to buy hard drugs to inject it into themselves. Yet every time you structure your life to conform to some unwritten social media rule, this is precisely what you're doing. This is what compels people to rent clothes and to borrow money to fund phone purchases.

Budgeting money and being smart with it does not mean you need to deny yourself these things. Instead, it's all about allocating your money in smart ways. This applies even if you're carrying debt. You don't have to say no to pleasurable experiences. What you need to do is prioritize well and act accordingly.

You'll learn how to do this further in this book.

Habits That You Need

If you want to manage your money well and increase it over time, you need to adopt certain habits. It's no secret that the habits that you practice everyday are what reflect who you really are. People can say whatever they want but it is their actions that count the most. A person who wears a fancy watch and claims to be on time is unreliable if they continuously show up late for their appointments.

We often value our perceptions more than reality. We lend more weight to what people say than what they do. This is what leads many people to believe that they're making changes as long as they say the right things. However, real change comes from what you do day in and day out.

In order to live the life you want, you'll need to link together a few habits that will help you build a good foundation that lasts a long time.

Habit #1 - Retirement Planning

Retirement seems to be a long time away, but it's important that you start allocating money towards it right now. Your 20s are often the best time in your life. You're still young enough to enjoy most things but are now getting paid a good amount of money. The whole world will seem to be accessible all of a sudden.

In this rush, it can be easy to ignore or neglect the need to save some money every month. You'll be tempted to think there's a lot of time and that you can always save some money next month. However, remember that you are your habits. If you're someone who kicks the can of saving down the road, this is what you'll become.

You'll be the person who hasn't saved any money for retirement and is facing the prospect of living at a lower standard of life than what they're used to. It's far easier to sacrifice today than to expect your older self to do so down the road.

Make it a point to list your retirement goals. Where do you want to live and how do you want to live? Keep in mind that your income needs will be greater once you're older thanks to the vagaries of life. Work backwards from those goals to see how much money you'll need to have saved. Read blogs and books that will educate you about how money grows over time and how much you can expect your savings to grow to at the end of a certain time period.

If all of this seems too much, simply set aside a certain amount of money into a separate account. Even if you can spare just $100, do so. Every little bit counts thanks to the power of compounding interest. Compound interest, or compounding, happens when your money grows at a fixed rate of interest over time. For example, if you invest $100 at 10% interest per year, you'll have $110 at the end of that period. Over the next year $110 will grow at 10% to yield $121. Then $121 grows at 10% and so on.

It's free money for you in the long run. This is how wealth is attained.

Habit #2 - Budgeting

Budgeting is simple and is yet complex at the same time. Making a budget is quite straightforward. All you need to do is use a spreadsheet or an app and list your expenses every month. It's a good idea to list your savings amount as well as any other contribution you're making towards a future purchase as an expense as well.

This will put you in the saving frame of mind and you won't be frivolous with your expenditures. The hard part is tracking and sticking to your budget. You'll walk past a fancy store and see a pair of shoes that you absolutely must have. Any concerns about your budget will evaporate in the rush that moment.

It's only after you take stock of things that you'll realize that those shoes have blown your budget. There are many apps that track your spending and help you categorize expenditures. However, none of these are a replacement for your own mind.

You need to prioritize spending your money in such a way that it grows over time. Money that grows will buy you more things in the future than cash right now. If sticking to your budget is such a problem then don't walk around with credit cards in hand. Instead, carry a fixed amount of cash and pay for everything using it.

This will get you thinking about the prices of the things you pay for and whether they're really worth the expense. Tracking your spending isn't easy, but keep working at it and you'll see results. It doesn't happen overnight, so let go of any such expectations you might have.

Instead, commit to getting on top of your budget and spending habits over the course of six months. Remember that your debt payments are an expense as well. Ideally, the debt payment will be the biggest expense on your budget. If this isn't the case, see if you can divert spending from other areas to pay down your debt as quickly as possible.

Once your debt is paid, this will result in a massive boost to your savings automatically.

Habit #3 - Set Goals

Do you want to be a millionaire? The truth is that if you budget and allocate your expenses well, you cannot help but become a millionaire. Here's how it works. If you can set aside $1,000 every month for 23 years and invest it in a simple index fund or exchange traded fund in the stock market, you'll have a million dollars.

The stock market has historically grown at a rate of 10% every year over the last 100 years. Despite the shocks to the American economy, the fact is that America's industries and businesses are unlikely to disappear overnight. This means you can expect this rate of growth on average in the future.

Can you set aside $1,000 after all of your expenses? If you don't have any debt, odds are good that you can. Can you see why paying your debt should be of the utmost priority? The $1,000 that goes towards paying off your debt principal could instead be going towards your million dollar fund.

A common question people ask is whether they ought to invest in stocks or real estate when they're still carrying other forms of debt. The answer is no. If you have debt, as much of your money as possible should go towards paying that debt down. Don't assume a mortgage under any circumstances.

This is because if you're carrying debt, the terms of your mortgage will cost you money. You'll receive worse interest rates that will only place a bigger burden on your cash flow. Instead, focus on eliminating debt and reduce any mortgage related expenses. You don't need to assume a mortgage in order to invest in real estate.

You can do this by investing in the stock market; debt is not the only means to buy a piece of property. You'll read about how some people own a million dollars' worth of property at the age of 25. Here's the truth: As long as the property is under mortgage, you don't own anything. The bank owns the place.

A mortgaged property that generates enough cash flow to make its interest payments is a good asset to carry. However, if something were to happen to that cash flow, you would spiral into massive debt quickly. Take all of these million dollar property claims with a pinch of salt. These people are either liars or they don't own the properties they claim to own thanks to having a mortgage on it. Remember that a heavy real estate portfolio carries its own risks due to the potential loss of cash flow from the property and changes to the housing or property market.

Habit #4 - Managing Money

People who are secure financially manage their money and enjoy doing so. Notice that I'm not saying they manage it "well." Once you begin to actively manage your money, you'll automatically do it well. It's how money management works. You'll understand how your money flows better once you engage with it and you'll automatically allocate it better.

Some people think they're bad at math and are intimidated by numbers. Fortunately, you only need basic arithmetic to manage your money well. Can you add? Can you subtract, multiple and divide? Yes? Congratulations, you're a money manager! Don't let your perceived lack of math skills stop you.

If you're someone who stays up at night wishing for a million dollars, understand that in order to be able to handle that much money, you need to first manage a dollar well. Once you manage a dollar well, manage $10, $100, and so on. You need to build your skills up until you can handle large amounts of money.

Money will not stay with you if you cannot manage it. Do you know that lottery winners are more likely to file for bankruptcy within three to five years after winning than the average American (Hess, 2017)? This is because they have no idea how to manage their winnings. Most lottery winners claim they regret not tearing up their winning ticket.

You need to make money management a priority. The good news is all it takes to do this is to stick to your budget and to then spend a few hours every month taking stock of what your money situation looks like. Did you spend within your limits? How much did you make? Did you save as much as you wanted?

That's all there is to it! You can add more goals on top of this such as increasing passive income and building an alternate source of money. However, it begins with those three fundamental questions. Ask yourself those three questions and you'll manage your money better than the average person.

Habit #5 - Flexibility and Growth

You're not going to keep earning the amount of money you're making right now. As you progress in your career, you'll likely make more money as your skills grow. As your money grows, you should add more goals to your financial plan. One goal I mentioned previously was passive income.

This is an important source of income since you don't need to work for it. You can earn passive income by either investing in the stock market or a savings account. You can also earn it by investing in a business that runs online automatically. This method requires more effort, but it demonstrates that there are endless opportunities for you to make money on the side.

All that matters is that you keep educating yourself about money management. This will give you the skills you need to handle increasing amounts of money. Once you have those skills, you won't find yourself scratching your head when the time comes to allocate it. If you don't practice money management, money that you haven't planned for will end up being spent on frivolous expenses. This leads you right back where you began.

Tips for Getting Out of Debt in Your 20s and 30s

Debt must be crushed. There, I said it. You need to adopt this mindset if you're serious about managing your money optimally. While you need to save some money that can help you tide over unexpected incidents in your life, the rest of your cash needs to be directed towards eliminating your debt as much as possible.

Here are a few tips that will help you crush debt.

Prioritize Fiscal Discipline

It all begins with your mindset and habits. If you make a decision to get on top of your money and to control it, you'll find yourself doing so automatically. While you will make mistakes along the way, you'll still be in a better position than not managing your money at all.

It will be tough for you to control yourself. Your brain will tell you that you're imprisoning yourself or that you're sacrificing far too much.

However, ask yourself what is more empowering: being debt free or having that shiny new phone and remaining in debt?

Discipline is all about prioritizing the things that truly matter to you. This is what leads to financial freedom.

Consolidate Your Debt

Consolidate your debt as much as possible. If you're carrying lots of credit card debt, transfer the balance to a card that has the lowest interest rate. Most card companies will allow you to transfer your debt balance for free.

Note that I'm not telling you to open a new credit card account for the sole purpose of consolidating debt. That's counter to your objectives. Instead, transfer it to one of your existing accounts. The same applies to student loan debt relief.

If you have more than one loan, try to consolidate it into a single payment. When paying off your loans, pay the one that has the highest interest off first. This will reduce the chances of the interest compounding and costing you even more money. The only exception is that you should pay off a full loan balance if you have enough money to do so.

Debt consolidation is extremely desirable because it will make your payment far more manageable. Instead of having to track multiple payment dates and debt balances, all you need to track is a single payment. Not all debts can be consolidated, but for ease of payment you should consolidate them as much as you can.

Pay Intelligently

The method I described in the previous section, paying off the highest interest debt first, is called the debt avalanche method. This prevents you from accumulating interest on top of unpaid interest. This amount will compound over time and your debt burden will increase if left unattended.

Often, people choose to pay the debt with the highest amount first. This isn't necessarily the wrong thing to do. However, if you miss a payment on higher interest debt, it will cost you more.

Try to pay down the principal as well as the interest portion of your debts when you make a payment. Make principal payments over and above the monthly payment and this will reduce your monthly debt payment. The only exception is if there's a prepayment penalty. This penalty is present in some mortgage contracts.

Develop a Side Gig

In this day and age, having a second source of income is imperative. If you're relying on a single source of income, you're one step removed from poverty. Multiple sources of income will better insulate you from adverse circumstances you can't control.

People often look at a second job as being something one takes on during hard times. You need to change your mindset with regards to this. A second job is an intelligent thing to do given the way the economy has been behaving over the past two decades. Corporations will not hesitate to sack you if their bottom line is under threat.

You need to develop a secondary source of income as quickly as possible to make sure your financial wellbeing isn't threatened. You'll learn all about developing side gigs later in this book.

Reduce Expenses

Building wealth is done by executing two things: reducing expenses and increasing income. Reducing expenses is a slightly pessimistic or negative way of looking at things. Taking this approach too far runs the risk of denying yourself the things you enjoy in the name of discipline.

Discipline isn't about denying or imprisoning yourself; it's about prioritizing your spending. When you're making smaller amounts of money, you'll make more of an impact by reducing your expenses than by making more money. What do I mean?

Let's say you make $2,000 per month and are paying rent of $1,000. This is 50% of your income. If you reduce your rental expense to $500, you've just saved an additional 25% of your income. If you were to invest $1,000 into a business that returns 20% (which is a very high return), you'll earn $200 which is 10% of your income. Which is better: earning an additional 25% through reducing expenses or earning 10% through investment?

Once your income grows, your investment returns will outweigh whatever savings you earn through reducing expenses. Until you reach a monthly income (after taxes) of $5,000 or so, it's best to focus on reducing expenses. Keep allocating money for investment after all of your payments are made, assuming you're debt free, but work on reducing your expenses as much as possible.

Build an Emergency Fund

You must always have an emergency fund. The problem with emergency funds is that it leaves you waiting for an emergency. Instead, reframe this as a financial freedom fund. If you have three months' worth of living expenses saved, you're free to loosen the reins a bit on your spending.

You're not completely dependent on your primary source of income now that you have a backup fund in place. Put these funds in a savings account or in certificates of deposit so that they earn interest and are easily accessible at the same time.

Typically, it's best to have six months' worth of expenses in the bank. You might also want to have an additional amount in place to account for unexpected expenditures.

Seek Help

It's impossible to know everything when you're just starting out. Reading a book such as this one is a great first step to take. If your credit situation happens to be extremely dire and if no amount of fixing seems to help improve it, consider counseling with a professional. It will cost you money upfront, but it will be money well spent.

There are a number of programs and consolidation options that a professional can walk you through. Instead of trying to do everything by yourself, you can use their help to make your financial situation a lot better.

Always look to invest in yourself and improve your knowledge. Times change and you'll need to change along with them. Constantly looking to improve your knowledge is the way to ensure you're not left behind.

Understand Your Credit Score

Your credit score is one of the most important numbers in your adult life. It defines how easy or hard your financial life is going to be. It's unfortunate that your creditworthiness is reduced to a number but that's just how it is.

The younger you are, the easier it is to repair your credit score. Focus on maintaining payments that reduce your debt. Make sure you have at least one credit account and immediately pay your purchases on it without carrying a balance forward. This will boost your creditworthiness.

The higher your credit score is, the cheaper it will be for you to borrow money. I've already highlighted how your credit score affects your ability to draw a mortgage. Even if you never have to borrow money in the future, a high credit score helps you apply for credit cards that give you truly amazing perks such as free flights, free food, and entertainment options. People with low credit scores do not qualify for these perks.

A good credit score will actually save you money in the long run. Make improving it as much as you can a point of action.

When followed together, all of these tips along with the previous material you've learned in this chapter will help you get out of debt. It won't happen overnight because you probably have certain spending habits that are draining your credit. However, the key thing to generate is awareness.

When you make becoming financially literate a goal, you'll see your financial situation improve over time.

Chapter 2:

Reducing Monthly Expenses

One half of reducing your debt burden and gaining control over your finances is reducing the amount of money you spend every month. This is a tricky thing to deal with because it's easy to go overboard and start denying yourself the things you enjoy.

Extreme expense reductions like these only result in a backlash against them. As a result, you'll find yourself going back to your old habits and that makes it tougher for you to get back to saving money. The key is to maintain a middle ground where you're not spending money frivolously, but at the same time you're not so tight fisted that you deny yourself things everyone enjoys.

If you're someone who has no idea where your money goes and you find yourself wondering where your paycheck went, this chapter is tailor made for you. Getting a handle of your expenses is a lot easier than it seems at first. Like everything else, it begins with taking the first step.

Budgeting 101

You might think you know budgeting but creating a budget and following one are two different things. The fact is that most people get creating budgets wrong, which makes following them even harder. For example, some people don't allocate an entertainment expense in their budget. As a result, they either deny themselves all forms of entertainment or go overboard with it since those expenses aren't being tracked.

Another common mistake is to try to fix rigid spending limits to line items. No one can accurately predict all of their expenses ahead of time. The key is to be as realistic as possible and to work forward from there. Some expenses, such as monthly rent, can be fixed with high accuracy. Others such as grocery and food are an estimate and will fluctuate.

Before addressing all of these issues, let's first take a look at which line items should be present on your budget, at a minimum.

Minimalist Budget

Here are the basic expenses that almost everyone incurs. Writing them down, either on paper or on a spreadsheet or an app, will help you track them. Whatever is tracked can be improved.

- Rent (if you have a mortgage, write that amount here)
- Food and drink
- Transportation (car payments, public transport costs, vehicle insurance)
- Health insurance
- Entertainment (you can include eating out under this category or under food expenses)
- Grooming
- Gym/fitness classes
- Other debt payments (student loans, credit card loans, etc.)
- Miscellaneous (a catch-all line item for unexpected and small expenses)

Here are some line items you must always have if you want to improve your financial life:

- Goal related savings contribution (I'll talk about these shortly)
- Long term savings contribution
- Self-improvement contribution
- Charity contribution
- Side hustle investment contribution
- Emergency fund contribution (this line item disappears if you have six months of living expenses saved)

When you put all of these together, you'll have a pretty lengthy budget list. The contribution line items are present to help you organize your plan for financial freedom. It helps you get excited about earning and managing your money. Budgets can turn into dreary and boring things because all you're tracking is your spending.

You're likely to get the impression that your money is constantly flowing away from you. Incorporating these contributions into your budget will help you become aware of how your money is working for you and shielding you. It brings a positive spin that will encourage you to find ways to increase your income.

From the expense portion of the budget, there are some items that are fixed. Rent/mortgage payments, fitness classes, transportation, and insurance expenses have largely or entirely fixed expenditures. These should be easy to pinpoint. Work towards reducing these as much as you can without causing yourself harm.

The line items dealing with entertainment, grooming, and groceries can vary. It's never a good idea to drastically reduce grocery expenses. Instead, place a floor and a ceiling on that expense. For example, you could fix a floor of $200 and a ceiling of $400 to it. Try to hit a middle ground of $300 per month spent on groceries so you're not veering towards the extreme.

Make it a point to spend a minimum of 10% of your after tax pay on entertainment options. If you're earning $2,000 every month, you can aim to spend at least $200 per month on entertainment. If you have student loan debt to clear, this becomes a maximum limit. Movie tickets, nights out on the town, eating outside your home, and buying yourself things you want but don't need come under this line item.

Grooming is important. You shouldn't walk around looking less than your best just because you're trying to save money. You don't need to splurge on celebrity stylists, but don't get your haircut from a blind guy with a pair of clippers either. If you're having a hard time figuring out this expense, fix a ceiling and a floor and hit the average.

If you genuinely enjoy spending time in a nail salon or in any other form of grooming, consider adding that to your entertainment expense.

The miscellaneous line item is the most important one. It will help you account for any overflow in expenditures. Create all of these in the budgeting method of your choice and designate limits for them. The miscellaneous line item is usually not more than 10% of your overall spending. So if you're spending $2,000 per month, it shouldn't exceed $200.

Emergency Fund Contribution

Now that the boring stuff is out of the way, let's talk about the line items that push you towards financial freedom. The first and most important of these is the emergency fund contribution. This is the most important payment you need to make after your debt payments.

If you're carrying debt, this is the only contribution you'll make until the debt is cleared. Your goal here is to save six months' worth of living expenses as cash. Open a savings account and contribute monthly amounts to it. Whenever you get paid, pay down your debt first and then transfer the contribution next. Whatever is left should pay for your expenses.

What if your contributions are tiny? If they are, then so be it. If all you can afford to transfer is a dollar, you should transfer that dollar. The action of working towards a goal is a powerful thing, and your mind will begin to generate ideas to increase that contribution. If you're struggling with money, the thought of having a backup of six months will excite you and you'll naturally work to increase the amount.

Remember that your objective with the debt payments is to reduce your principal and not just make interest payments. Let's say you get paid $2,000 and that your consolidated debt payment that reduces your principal is $1,000. Pay this amount and then subtract your expenses from $1,000. You'll know what your expenses ideally are from your budget. Let's say this is $800.

Transfer the remaining $200 to your emergency fund as a contribution. During some months you'll have higher expenditures, so this amount may decrease. As long as you're contributing something, you're doing great.

Once you have six months' worth of cash on hand, you'll transfer one month's expenses, including all debt payments according to your budget, to your checking account and live off that money. When your paycheck arrives, you'll directly transfer that to your savings account. The following month, you'll once again withdraw one month's worth of expenses and live on that.

This is called cycling your money and it's an extremely powerful action. You'll disconnect from having to rely on your paycheck to pay your bills. If this sounds like a pipe dream to you at the moment, remember that all you need to do is to contribute towards your emergency fund. Don't worry about how long it'll take to get there.

As long as you do it, you'll arrive at your goal eventually. So start that process by taking action.

Goal Related Contributions

Everyone has things they want to save for. It could be downpayment on a property or it could be something as simple as a vacation. I'd like to point out once more that as long as you're carrying unpaid debt, you should not be establishing this line item. You'll only have expenses and the emergency fund.

The goal related contribution can come from the amount of money you were previously paying towards your debt. Write down what your goal is and set up a little fund for it. You can have multiple goals here. You could save up for a downpayment on a mortgage and you can have a contribution that goes towards buying those really expensive shoes that you adore.

Long Term Savings Contribution

This is an extremely important line item. Your long term savings is the money that you'll invest in the stock market and other financial vehicles that will compound and grow over time. This money should be at least 10% of your after tax pay. If you can make this at least 30% once you've cleared your debt, you're going to be in good shape.

This cash won't sit in your bank account. It'll probably lie as a balance in your brokerage account or in a retirement account. Once you're debt free, make it a point to contribute as much as you can to this account.

A point to note: This line item does not become active unless you're free of debt and have established an emergency fund and are cycling your money. Without these things in place, there's no point in you trying to invest because your debts will drain whatever gains you make.

Side Hustle and Self Improvement Contribution

Your side hustle contribution is a fund that can amount to $2,000 or even $5,000. This is the money you'll have as cash to invest in learning all about a profitable side hustle that can be turned into a stream of passive income. It does not become active until you're debt free and have an emergency fund along with cycling your money.

You can contribute an amount that feels right to you to fund this contribution. You can stop contributions once you've reached the goal of $5,000. The good news is that a lot of side hustles these days don't cost a lot of money. For example, building an influencer account on Instagram doesn't have to cost money.

However, it takes time and a lot of effort. A side hustle fund can help you shortcut that process. Instead of building your own account, buy an influencer account for a sum of cash. Charge people for sponsored posts and you'll recover your money in a few months. Even better, you can sell products to this audience such as t-shirts and other affiliate related products.

This makes such investments great because they turn into money machines overnight. I'll discuss this in more detail later in this book. For now, understand that it's better to allocate money to buying your way into an income stream than to try and create one from scratch.

You could create a side hustle that can pay you from the start. Taking surveys, quizzes, and so on can pay you some cash that you can use. You could write on the side or work as a translator or as an English teacher. This contribution funds potential passive income streams down the road.

Self-improvement refers to educating yourself. All successful people read and you should spend time reading everyday. If you can't afford to buy books, read them online. Once your debt is cleared, dedicate a portion of your after tax income towards building a fund for courses you can take and books you can read.

Ideally, 10% of your income would be contributed to this fund, but your individual situation will dictate how much you can afford. Education is free these days thanks to the internet. YouTube is full of tutorials, so spend some time everyday learning new skills and improving old ones.

Websites such as Udemy help you learn new skills that you can then use to build new side hustles that increase your income.

Charity

Dedicate a portion of your income for donating to charitable causes. As tough as your current living situation might be, remember that there are those who have it far worse. So volunteer your time and contribute whatever you can to make their lives a bit better.

Using Apps

The great thing about using apps is that you'll be able to automate your budget goals. You'll need to spend some time categorizing your spending, but the visual data that you'll receive, as well as the time you'll spend categorizing expenses, will help you get a clear picture of where your money is going.

Mint is one of the oldest apps in the space and is the best for overall management. It connects with a wide variety of bank and investment accounts so using it is easy. Mint's best feature is its data analytics that give you a variety of charts to help you visualize your spending.

If debt reduction is your primary aim, You Need a Budget or YNAB is your best bet. You can set up debt related goals and YNAB will help you figure out the best payment method and allocations that will result in the quickest reduction of debt. You can also try other apps such as Toshl and Pocketguard.

If the thought of connecting your financial accounts to a third party app worries you, tracking your expenses manually is the best choice. Create your line items in a spreadsheet and track expenses manually. Keep your receipts and enter expenses diligently.

At the end of every month, or on the day you get paid, take stock of what your finances look like. If you want to examine them in between, feel free to do so. The more interest you display in managing your money, the more your money will work for you. Once you start saving money and see the passive interest payments build, you'll be energized by this and will automatically start making more money.

It all begins with a budget so once you're done reading this section, go ahead and create a budget right now. Use whatever tools you need and put the advice in this section into immediate action.

Reducing Expenses

Once your budget is set you'll have a clear picture of which expenses need to reduce. The incorrect way to approach reducing your spending is to try to do it all at once. This only results in half-baked results that are unsustainable over the long term. Here are some tips to help you keep your expenses in check over the long term.

Set Realistic Goals

Everything begins with your goals. Your goals are roadmaps that will guide you throughout your journey. This much is obvious. However, your goals also dictate how you feel about your achievements. For example, if your goal was to go from a place of spending $500 over budget to coming in $500 under budget, a spending reduction of $100 will seem like nothing.

However, if your goal was to simply spend as much as you had allocated for the month, then a $100 reduction will seem massive. It's all about perspective. The best way to go about achieving your desired goals is to set them incrementally. Reduce overspending gradually instead of trying to undo it in one swoop.

For example, your first goal should be to set a budget and track your expenses diligently for a week. If you're using an app, you could earmark an hour every week to categorize your expenses. Do this for two weeks and then for a month. At the end of the month, look at how much money you spent and whether you went over budget.

If you went over budget by $500, resolve to reduce it to $400 next month. Identify the things you could cut back on and put these into action over the next month. Meanwhile, continue to follow your habit of tracking your expenses and categorizing them for an hour every week.

Over time, you'll find that the sum of these habits will add up to a much larger whole than their parts. You'll create momentum in your life and you'll end up reducing your spending automatically.

Rely on Yourself

If you're someone who's experienced financial difficulties and money shortfalls, your default approach might be to rely on your parents or on your friends to lend you some money. While it's nice to have backups in place, this should not be your default position every time you get into financial trouble.

Instead, resolve to be self-reliant. You might not have confidence in your own abilities to handle money at this point, but these habits can be learned. Look at the previous tip for an example. You'll begin with a basic task of creating a budget line by line. Once this is done, you need to spend just an hour every week to categorize expenses.

That's less than 10 minutes everyday. Anyone can do that. You don't need a financial gene or some special gift to be good with money. Your aim isn't to be the world's foremost expert on money management. You just need to know where your money goes and where it comes from. Achieving this state is quite easy once you dig into the details.

The best part is that as you begin to manage your money, your confidence will grow. You'll find yourself not having to rely on others to give you money, which will make you start believing in yourself. This virtuous circle will bring even more success with money and in curtailing your damaging spending habits.

So take that first step and resolve to rely on yourself no matter what.

Use Tools

You cannot do everything by yourself or maintain spending records in your head. Someone who's been tracking their expenses on a daily basis for over a decade will struggle to do this. As someone who's just beginning their budgeting journey, it's unrealistic for you to expect this.

People who think they can keep all of their spending amounts in their memory are simply being lazy and are giving into their old selves. Your mind is resistant to change and will regularly draw you back into the past and into your damaging spending habits. Avoid this by reminding yourself of the fact that you're not self-reliant.

Download apps or maintain a spreadsheet so that you can track your expenses. Use the method that is easiest for you to maintain. Some people find it easier to enter expenses manually and create a pivot table in a spreadsheet program. Others find apps a lot more convenient.

I've already highlighted the best apps you can use, and I encourage you to make use of them. Do what's necessary to change.

Cover the Essentials

I've already mentioned the first things you need to do when you receive your paycheck or income stream. You need to first pay down your debt and then pay your essential expenses. Whatever is left over goes to your emergency fund. Notice that I said "essential" expenses.

Technically speaking, food is an essential expense but that's not the kind of essential I'm talking about here. What I'm talking about are those expenses that attract late fees and cost you more money to clear if you're late paying them. Rent/housing payments, utility bills, and other debt related payments are essential.

Pay these as quickly as possible. Look to reduce these expenditures as much as you can. Negotiate to decrease your rent with your landlord when you have money to pay them the full amount. Most people negotiate when they desperately need the reduction; this puts them in an inferior position when it comes to negotiations.

Instead, ask for a reduction when you don't need one. That way, even if they decline your request, you'll not be hit too hard by it. If they agree, you've scored a win! If your landlord rents a bunch of properties in the same building, work with the other tenants to request a rent decrease.

Replacing a bunch of tenants is painful for most landlords and they'll be willing to accept small decreases in rent to avoid the hassle. Use this to your advantage and negotiate from a position of strength. Be realistic in your requests. Remember that your landlord is running a business and needs to make money as well.

Combining utility bills or eliminating services you don't need can reduce your expenses. Choose a cheaper phone plan if you can and choose streaming services instead of more expensive cable options.

In some areas, choosing to use your phone's internet at home instead of a broadband connection makes more sense and reduces expenses. If you're someone who loves reading, you might not even need a cable or streaming connection. Examine your expenses and work to reduce them as much as possible.

Wants and Needs

Can you differentiate between your wants and needs? If you're reading this book, you probably have difficulties with this. Your needs are things that are essential for your survival. You need shelter, clean water, food and clothes. You also need entertainment options to reduce stress.

There are varying degrees of expenditures within these categories that can turn a need into a want. You need food but do you really need to eat a lavish meal everyday? You need shoes but do you really need that pair of Louboutins? Figuring out the threshold between your needs and wants is crucial if you wish to save money.

A good way to figure this out and to enforce discipline is to fix an entertainment expense. Use this money to address your wants. You'll find that a reduced degree of spending will satisfy you. For example, you might crave a pizza every day. Clearly this is a want and isn't a need.

Spending some money once a week to eat pizza will help you realize that you don't need an entire pie to satisfy your craving. A single slice will start doing the trick for you and you'll end up spending less. Similarly, cutting down on entertainment expenses will help you realize which things bring you true pleasure. Unsurprisingly, these options won't cost you too much.

It takes work to figure out your thresholds. Examine how you feel after you've indulged in something. Do you feel immense relief and then nothing at all after consuming something? This indicates your desire was a want and not a need. Needs don't produce extreme emotion within us. They usually leave us feeling content and satisfied as opposed to euphoric or strained.

Limit Media Consumption

As you've already learned and have experienced, everyone is selling you something or the other these days. Social media companies exist to sell you stuff. How else can they make money? They actively limit posts and feeds from your true friends and push money making nonsense to you all the time.

It's easy to get caught up with the world of social media. One of the basic urges that every human being has is to fit in. Even the so-called lone wolves and introverts have a desire to fit in somewhere. It's how we're built. This leads us to cave into peer pressure and to follow the herd in the hopes that we'll fit in better.

Ultimately, everyone realizes that behaving this way is nonsensical. The lucky ones realize it earlier in their lives than the unlucky ones. Here's an experiment you should conduct. Block all of your access to social media (no exceptions!) and use a blocking extension to limit your access to certain websites (news, current events, opinionated blogs, "thought" blogs, etc.).

If you watch TV, avoid programs that deal with the following: politics, gossip, foreign affairs, finance and news. If this means you can only watch a deer prancing around in the Serengeti then so be it. Do this for two days and take stock of how you feel.

Notice how much lower your anxiety is upon waking up. The world will seem to be a much better place once you do this for a long enough period. At some point you should even consider ditching your smartphone, but there's no need to get that drastic at this point.

Entertain Intelligently

I've already mentioned how limiting your entertainment expenses will open your eyes to the things you truly enjoy. The point of entertainment is to reduce stress. It isn't to show off to other people how wealthy or cool you are. Most entertainment venues project this vibe because they're also in the business of selling something to you.

People mindlessly spend money in the hopes of impressing some stranger they'll never see again. A lot of nightlife entertainment options tap into your need to fit in and deliver huge doses of peer pressure. Take a step back and review what exactly it is that these options add to your life. If you're unable to do this or feel you need the release that these venues provide, you should limit your spending.

There are many ways of scoring free entertainment. If you live near a college town, fairs and other events hosted in the local community will offer you free entertainment. Street fairs and food festivals are great options. In addition to this, check out websites such as Meetup or start your own social club to meet new people.

Attending language exchanges is a great way to meet people from different parts of the world and to also help someone speak English or whichever language is being spoken. You can also use websites such as iTalki to communicate with people in a different language. This will jog your brain and give you free mental exercise.

When meeting with friends, consider meeting at a coffee shop instead of a bar. A coffee shop is somewhere you can hang out for the price of a single cup of coffee whereas you'll be tempted to overspend at a bar on alcohol and food. This doesn't mean you should cut this option away completely. It's just that moderation in everything is good practice.

View the Long Term

We're often guilty of sacrificing long term benefits for short term pleasure. It's how human beings are built. We cannot forecast anything with reasonable accuracy and plans that rely on long term goals cannot be visualized with high degrees of confidence. It takes practice and training for us to be able to do this.

When the time comes for you to choose to violate your discipline and spend on something that brings you short term pleasure, you should take a step back and ask yourself whether this is the right thing to do or not. Remind yourself of the things you'll potentially be giving up to indulge in this want.

A good rule of thumb is to ask yourself whether you can really afford the thing you want. If you can't buy it twice, you can't afford a want. By buying it twice, I'm referring to the amount of money you have left after all of your allocations and expenses are paid for. Can you buy those fancy shoes after your money is fully allocated and put to work?

If not, you can't afford it. If it fits your entertainment expense then go for it. However, keep in mind that exhausting your entire expense on a single item is unwise. The point of these rules is to get you thinking about where your money ought to be allocated and what brings you the greatest amount of long term utility.

Once you start thinking this way and making these decisions you'll get better at it, and soon you'll execute them effortlessly.

Cash Cleanse

Alternatively called a cash diet, this is when you pay all of your expenses using just cash. Handing cash over physically makes spending seem much more real for us. You'll also need to think of your expenses in advance when paying for everything in cash, so you'll become more conscious of where your cash is going.

In this age of contactless and digital payments, a cash cleanse might not be the most practical solution. However, do it as much as possible and you'll see yourself reducing your spending drastically.

Shop Smarter

Deals exist everywhere. Check out websites such a Groupon and coupons.com for deals on groceries and other daily essentials. When buying essentials such as soap or toothpaste, buy them in bulk from a big box retailer. When buying electronics or other specialty items, wait for the times of the year when they go on sale.

Another tactic you can use when visiting an electronics store is to offer to pay them in cash. Paying for something in cash usually results in a discount. Talk to the manager to see if there are any offers or discounts available. When you go grocery shopping, make a list ahead of time of all the things you need.

This will prevent you from overspending on things you don't need. Wandering around grocery store aisles is the easiest way to end up buying things that will push you over your budget limit. It's easy to go overboard with reducing spending. Don't sacrifice quality in favor of saving money.

Buying clothes from Walmart is a lot cheaper but you should still spend money on professional looking clothes from a good store. Wearing cheap clothes to an important business meeting could make you lose credibility.

Buy your food as fresh as possible. Processed foods are much cheaper and won't strain your wallet. However, they're extremely unhealthy for you in the long run. Instead, learn how to cook fresh food and cook them in batches. This will ensure you'll have tasty meals at all times and will be eating healthy as well. A top tip when shopping for groceries is to eat prior to shopping.

If you shop for food when hungry, you'll end up buying items such as chocolates or sweets that will give you a quick carb boost but won't fill your stomach or provide nutrition. I'm not saying you should cut chocolate out altogether, but if you buy them it should be part of a planned purchase.

Learning to cook at home will save you more money than anything else and will also ensure you eat healthy. Even meals cooked at healthy restaurants have a bunch of stuff in them that aren't good for your health. Avoid all of these problems by cooking at home. Buy a large pot or an oven and cook your food in advance.

Prep your meals ahead of time and pack your food in boxes. If you're used to eating out all the time, start off by eating one home cooked meal everyday. Increase this to two per day the following week until you reduce the number of meals you eat outside to one every week. Think of this as your cheat meal and indulge yourself. Make space for it within your entertainment expense.

Buy Used

You should avoid buying things new as much as possible. This doesn't apply to assets that make you money. However, you should buy items such as vehicles and even clothes in a used condition. These days there are many thrift and vintage stores that offer high quality clothing that have been previously worn.

You don't want to sacrifice quality for money so make sure the clothing fits you well and that you look well groomed. When it comes to vehicles, buying used is a no-brainer. In fact, you need to avoid assuming car loan debt if you have outstanding student loan debt.

A new car purchase means you'll end up paying a lot more for something that declines in value. It's estimated that a new car loses up to a third of its value the minute it's driven off the dealer's lot. This is doubly the case when it comes to luxury cars. The people who drive these cars either rent them for entertainment purposes or have enough money to render that expense negligible.

If you're in the market for a car, buy one that works and is available cheap. You're not going to turn heads driving it but that's not the point. If you have to assume a loan, pay it down as much as possible and to the extent where you can get rid of the loan within a year.

This will mean you'll be shopping for cars around the $10,000 mark or less. There are great deals on used cars all the time so do your research and negotiate with the dealer. A common mistake people make is to think of a car purchase as being a monthly payment. They look at their car payment and think it costs "just $300."

Since they make $2,000 or more per month this doesn't register as a huge expense. However, this payment continues for a long time and costs them money in the long run. It's a classic case of putting short term gratification ahead of long term benefit.

Above all else, don't put a new purchase on credit cards and think you can pay it off later. As I mentioned previously, you should not have a credit card if you're carrying student loan debt. Once you get rid of your debt you can carry one to maintain your credit score, but make sure you pay it off immediately.

Chapter 3:

Building Wealth - Ways to Start

Earning More

Saving money can be a dreary subject. It's far more exciting to talk about how you can make more money. This is what excites us after all. Remember that when your expenses are high in comparison to your income, you'll save more money by reducing expenses. Once your income starts increasing, you'll make more money by investing it intelligently.

You'll learn all about investing in later chapters. For now, you need to learn how you can make more money. The holy grail of earning money is passive income. As explained earlier, this is income that is disconnected from the amount of time you spend creating it. Passive income generators include savings accounts, stock market investments, and fully managed rental properties.

The key thing to note here is that income comes in two forms. There's capital gains and cash flow. When you're looking to increase your income from a lower standard you want to focus on cash flow. Capital gains build your wealth immensely but you can't use that cash in the interim.

For example, if you save $1,000 to invest in stocks that don't pay you anything, it won't make much of a difference to your spending or saving habits if the stock increases in prices. It could increase by 20% over a year, but that cash is unrealized since you aren't getting paid. Your expenses are still the same and your cash on hand is the same.

This is why investing in non cash producing assets is not an optimal use of your cash when you don't have much to invest. It's far better to take that $1,000 and invest it in an online business venture that can make you a 100-500% return. Such astronomical returns are possible because the investment amounts are low.

Once you have steady cash flow producing assets, focus on generating capital gains. You can afford to leave that money alone and have it grow over time since your cash flow producing assets will help you pay for your expenses easily.

So with this preliminary information in mind, the first step for you to take is to monetize the things you already have.

Monetize Existing Resources

Too many people jump directly to money making ideas and don't take the time to first look at what they already have. The mindset of looking to monetize what you have will open your mind to potential money making ideas. Who knows, you might even want to develop one of them as a side gig.

The most obvious place to begin is in your closet. Adopt a minimalist approach to your possessions. If you haven't worn something for over a year and don't see an immediate need for it, consider selling it. If no one will buy it, donate it to the Salvation Army and get a receipt. You can use this receipt to claim a tax deduction when you file your taxes.

Next, you might own a car and you've just read all about how cars lose value. Turning this depreciating asset into an income producing one is quite straightforward. For starters you could moonlight as an Uber driver. If you happen to live in a big city, surge pricing will ensure you'll make a good amount of money ferrying passengers.

The best part is that you can choose to stop when you wish. Remember, this money isn't being made with the intention of creating a side gig. It's to simply reduce the debt burden you're carrying with your car loan currently. If you enjoy driving for a service like Uber, you can certainly turn it into a side gig. However, this is not the primary aim of this action.

There are other services that allow you to monetize your car. Turo, for example, allows you to place your car for rent and pays you when people rent it for however long they need it. You could also allow people to advertise their business on your car. As a mobile billboard, your car offers excellent exposure for businesses.

Your home is another place that costs you money. If you're unfortunate enough to have a mortgage along with being saddled by student debt, it's imperative for you to produce cash from your property. Consider moving your possessions into a room or two rooms and making the remaining bedrooms available for rent.

The rental cash flow will reduce the debt burden massively. It'll also help pay for any maintenance or repairs you need to carry out around the place. This method is often referred to as house hacking. It's when a person reduces or has their mortgage payment paid for by the rental cash flow they generate.

If you're renting a place from a landlord, you should check that they're okay with you subleasing the place. If you're renting an apartment, ask if there is a way you could sublease a portion of it. Landlords in bigger cities are usually fine with this. They'll expect a cut of the additional payment from the sublessee.

You can use the money earned from this sublease to decrease your rental payment burden. For example, if you're paying $1,000 per month for rent, you could sublease a portion of the property for $400. This reduces your rental payment per month to $600. Offer to manage listings for your landlord through Airbnb as well.

Many landlords are looking for help to reduce vacancies. If you show them you can sublease their property effectively, you could get them to pay you to manage their listings and live for free. It might be a long shot but it's one worth taking.

Your old possessions can be sold on eBay pretty easily. A good way of making money is to take a look at auctions that are about to expire on eBay. Note the price at which the product is selling and look at its price on Amazon. If it's cheaper on Amazon, you could buy it and list it for an auction.

You'll have to take care of shipping fees and so on but it's a good way to make some additional cash every month. Some people even expand this to a side gig. There aren't too many bargains you can find doing this, but this is a great way to make a little additional cash every month.

Another viable method is to use your internet browsing skills to get paid. Websites such as usertesting.com and userfeel.com pay you to test other people's websites. The work is intermittent, but you can sign up to their mailing list to earn a few bucks every week testing websites and recording your thoughts on their design.

Many people advise you to take surveys but this is a terrible idea. These surveys don't pay you enough money and take a considerable amount of time. They're also an unreliable source of income since the money you'll make depends heavily on your location. Instead of wasting your time filling these out, use the methods I've listed above.

Remember we're still talking about monetizing what you already have. These methods can be turned into side businesses, but there are better businesses out there for you to explore. The cash flow that these methods produce serve to reduce the burden your expenses place on you.

If you can manage to earn 30% of your expenses through these methods, you will free up your main source of income for investment opportunities or debt payments. For example, if your expenses amount to $2,000 per month and you can earn $600 driving an Uber or subletting your living space, you're doing very well.

Building Income Streams - Preliminary Work

Before we get into specific ideas to build income streams, it's important for you to learn the correct mindset with which you need to approach these opportunities. Many people approach money making ideas with a desperate mindset. This is understandable. They're in a tough situation and need ideas to dig themselves out of a hole.

This makes them easy prey to scammers. When it comes to most internet marketers, it's safe to assume they're a fraud until they've proven themselves to not be one. There are many ways to make money online and even the scammer might be successful using whatever product they're advertising. This doesn't mean you can make money though.

The internet business space is a fast moving one. Many business models have an expiration date on them. For example, dropshipping was a hot business idea back in 2015. Many people jumped on it and made a lot of money. When the business model began facing backlash from consumers, these lucky entrepreneurs turned to selling dropshipping courses.

Similarly, Amazon self-publishing was a golden business opportunity between 2016-2018. Literally anyone could make money during this time with a little bit of work. However, these days it requires a lot of effort due to the changes Amazon has made. There is no dearth of courses on offer though.

It's still possible to make money executing these business ideas. However, the learning curve is a lot steeper now and the existing players have a huge advantage. When it comes to online business models, if your business doesn't deliver value to the customer, it's not going to work.

This sounds like an obvious statement but many courses adopt a different approach. For example, it was possible during the initial days of dropshipping to deliver the product of the customer after a month. Try to do that these days and your customer will sue you. Yet, you'll find gurus selling such tactics in their courses. What's more, they'll charge you $10,000 for the privilege.

Any online guru or self-proclaimed mentor who sells consulting sessions for five figures or even for $5,000 is probably a scam artist. They want you to believe that making money is hard and that it takes special knowledge.

This is not the case at all. It's just a marketing tactic they use to convince you that you need their services. Some of these so-called mentors insist on being called honorary terms and build cult-like followings. Their videos are full of flashy cars and gorgeous women. Both the women and cars are rented though, so don't fall for these claims.

The best example of this is the marketer Tai Lopez who famously rented a Beverly Hills mansion for an hour or so along with a

Lamborghini and a few models he found on Craigslist. Lopez has managed to sell over a million dollars' worth of courses to gullible people who think he's some sort of a genius.

However, Lopez (who sells real estate investment courses) doesn't even know what a cap rate is and cannot define that term. This is something every newbie to real estate investing knows, yet this self-proclaimed guru cannot define it. Despite all of this, Lopez continues to sell his courses and people continue to believe he's genuine. It just goes to show how many desperate people are out there.

Another great example is the former scam artist Jordan Belfort. Belfort has publicly apologized for his actions which led to defrauding over 100 million dollars from investors. He felt so much remorse for his actions that he had no problems with Hollywood glorifying his scams and even wrote two books on the topic. There was even a sequel that was planned but thankfully it didn't make the cut.

Belfort now sells courses and seminars and is an "expert" on sales. Of course, he exhorts people to not use it for bad purposes and to only use his tactics for good. Meanwhile he continues to resist the justice system's attempts to recoup the losses his investors faced from the millions in royalties he's earned.

Understand that it is possible to get rich quickly. However, you don't get rich quickly by investing in get rich quick schemes. Any scheme that presents itself as being extremely complex or as being brilliant is actually quite simple. A quick search on Reddit and YouTube will reveal what it's all about.

Instead of focusing on getting rich quickly, focus on the processes that will make you money. Learn these processes well and see whether they provide people with any value. Unless you're providing customers with value, you're not going to get paid. It really is that simple.

Here are a few telltale signs of a fraudulent get rich quick scheme:

- It costs an exorbitant amount of money (over $5,000).

- The person or people promoting it have zero or low web presence.
- Their channels are full of fake engagement such as paid comments or likes.
- They refer to themselves as "guru" or "sifu" or any Eastern philosophical terms.
- They expect you to sell their courses to the people you know.
- They talk a lot about brand building despite not having one of their own.
- Excessive amounts of fast cars and other shiny objects in their marketing material.
- They make more money from selling courses than executing what they teach.
- They push pyramid schemes or multi-level marketing schemes.
- They're disrespectful or have an air of being better than you.
- They've been featured on the YouTube channel Coffeezilla, which exposes scam artists and gives a bunch of helpful tips on how to avoid them.
- They operate in a space where success is tough but claim to have a secret or patented system.
- They cannot produce records. Digital screenshots can be manipulated. If you cannot see them login to their dashboards or accounts, it's not real.
- This one applies to stock trading gurus: They claim to come from the hedge fund world but cannot produce a copy of their securities license or fund license. They do not have audited track records and refuse to share them.
- Something feels "off" about them. Your emotional instincts will inform you well in advance if you took the time to listen to them.

As you benign exploring money making ideas, keep all of these points in mind. You'll save yourself a ton of money and avoid being manipulated by these people.

The Best Ways to Build Wealth

The wealth building methods outlined here will take different amounts of time. Some will give you overnight results while some will take a few years. Some will give you a small and steady cash flow while others will give you tons of cash.

A good approach for you to pursue is wealth building that can be turned passive as much as possible. This is what truly frees up your time and your wealth will compound.

Microinvesting Apps

This is a basic money making strategy that everyone should be using. Apps such as Acorns round your purchases up to the nearest dollar and invest the difference in a diversified fund in the stock market. For example, if you purchased something for $2.51, the app takes 49 cents and invests it in a diversified exchange traded fund.

I'll explain what an exchange traded fund is later in the book. Micro investing is a great way for you to automate your investing and thanks to you investing mere pennies, it's something that happens on autopilot. It's a great way to begin investing. These days brokers don't charge any fees for transacting in the market, so it's an excellent way to invest small sums and generate passive income.

Granted, this method will never make you rich by itself. However, it's a great way to get your passive income ball rolling. Every journey has to start somewhere and you lose literally nothing through this method. So why not implement it?

Search for a Better Job

In the rush of trying to make more money, we often neglect the thing that makes money in the first place. There's nothing wrong with holding down a job. A lot of internet entrepreneurs will scoff at you and tell you you're working for a "master" and so on. However, you can be an entrepreneur and maintain a job that you enjoy working at.

You might be underpricing yourself in the market. People often don't negotiate enough when coming out of college, which puts them into a fixed bracket as far as their first employer is concerned. One of the best ways to increase your salary is to network. If you happen to be shy, then the great news is that websites such as LinkedIn have made networking extremely simple.

LinkedIn is perhaps the most useful of all social media networks. It's where your professional profile lives. Many recruiters scour LinkedIn for candidates. Maintain an active profile and optimize it for the keywords linked to your profession. Choose a professional profile photo and describe what it is you do.

Connect with as many people as possible. Many people make the mistake of connecting only with those they already know. Reach out to those who are in the same line of work but in different companies. Send them a message telling them you'd like to connect and they'll respond back.

Share interesting content on LinkedIn. This is as simple as searching for relevant news and clicking the share button with your thoughts added to it. Leave comments on the posts of those you connected with. All of this takes no more than an hour every day. You can do it during your lunch break and after you've returned from work.

You might be scared to advertise that you're looking for work at other organizations if you've connected with your boss. LinkedIn has privacy settings that limits what can be viewed by your contacts. Secondly, the best jobs don't tend to be advertised. Instead, message someone at a firm you'd like to work and tell them what you do.

Don't ask them for a job or anything of the sort. If and when a job opening becomes available, odds are good that they'll message you before advertising it. Not all jobs lend themselves well to online networking. Sometimes it's better to attend in-person networking events.

Every major city has these meetings going on so make it a point to attend them. You could even attend job fairs and pass your resume out. Some of the best prospects tend to come from trade shows and events. Again, the key is to present yourself as someone who's testing the waters. Don't present yourself as someone who's desperate for a job.

No one wants to hire somebody desperate after all.

Ask for a Raise

While you're searching for other opportunities, ask your boss for a raise. If you've never done this before it will be nerve wracking. However, it's something you must do in-person. Do not ask for a raise over email or other electronic communication.

If you finish a job successfully, make sure you email your boss and cc relevant people letting them know you've finished the work and have delivered it. You don't need to promote yourself excessively or obscenely but having it on the record helps.

Many people, especially introverts, prefer to work in silence and hope their boss recognizes them. This is Alice in Wonderland type thinking. Your boss has their own problems and isn't your friend. Their job is to pay you as little money as possible while keeping you happy and their boss happy. They're far more concerned with how they're being perceived and don't have time to treat you specially.

Thus, make sure you document all of your efforts. Get things in writing as much as possible and don't be afraid to say no. It's ironic but people who value their time and set boundaries are viewed as being better workers than those who say yes all the time. Don't be a pushover.

You're not going to lose your job if you say no a few times. If your boss gives you trouble for declining excessive requests, then it's time to find a new boss.

Schedule a meeting with your boss ahead of time and prepare your pitch. That's right. This is a pitch, it isn't a record of the things you've done. Research what the average pay rate is for your job and your industry and pitch accordingly. Pitching unrealistic numbers only presents you as being out of touch.

When pitching, it's easy to fall into the trap of listing your achievements. The initial reaction to this list of achievements is "so what?" Your boss isn't concerned with how great you are. They're far more concerned with your utility with regards to their professional life. Focus your pitch efforts on how you're making their lives easier.

Point out how you're reducing the time they spend supervising certain tasks or how you dealt with issues beforehand and stopped them from becoming a problem. If your job involves efficiency, point out how much money you saved the business. Any money you save gets rolled into your boss' record so it makes them look good as well.

Whatever you do, don't threaten to quit. This is childish and you'll leave them with a bad impression. If you're rejected, seek alternative offers. Schedule another meeting with your boss and let them know of it. If they match or better the offer, stay. If they don't, quit. That's the best way to handle job changes.

Freelancing

We're now leaving the realms of your current job and venturing into side hustles. Freelancing makes the most sense for a lot of people. It's a happy middle ground between their day job and a business. Freelancing in your area of expertise is the easiest way to begin a side hustle.

You could advertise your services to existing clients or ask for referrals. More often than not, customers need additional services that companies don't provide. This could be a great way for you to establish your own client base. Just make sure your company is okay with you doing this.

You should also be careful utilizing company resources to develop any product. Such products technically belong to the company and not to you. This is especially the case if you're developing software solutions to address current customer problems. Separate your activities from that of the company completely in order to protect your rights.

If your day job doesn't lend itself to freelancing opportunities, consider turning one of your hobbies into a side hustle. For example, if you love writing you could work for a content mill and earn some income on the side. Teaching English is also a popular side hustle for a lot of people.

There is a huge demand for skilled English language teachers and signing up through a platform to teach is easy. If you have teaching experience you can sign up through websites like iTalki and verbalplanet. Alternatively you could work through an agency that will take a cut of your earnings but will likely provide steady work.

Skills such as transcription are also heavily in demand especially in the legal and medical field. You can use your spare time to easily earn an additional $500-$1,000 transcribing legal and medical procedures. All freelancing side hustles need some time to develop. It's best to give yourself a year or so to really make a success of it.

Graphic design is an area that's always in demand. Speaking of demand, there's no shortage of it for computer developers. Learning programming is easy these days thanks to websites such as Udemy and Codecademy. Most firms that hire developers aren't concerned with educational qualifications beyond knowledge of the language you'll be programming.

Learning programming will also open up a ton of other fields for you such mobile app development and so on. Websites such as Toptal are a great resource to use for freelancing programmers to find work.

There are many other websites such as Fiverr and Upwork, but these are a terrible proposition for freelancers. These result in a race to the bottom for the most part.

Instead, it's much better to look for side gigs on websites such as AngelList that host a wide variety of listings from startups. You can also network on LinkedIn to find people in your target industry and find potential clients among them. It takes time but it's a great way to build credibility on the side.

Driving an Uber or Lyft can also be a side hustle if you enjoy doing it. Make sure you run the numbers properly to make sure you can actually make money doing this. It's a great way to monetize your car and have it generate additional cash. There is no limit to the kind of services you can provide after your work is done. All you need to do is make sure you pick something that you enjoy doing and that pays you well in return for the services you render.

The world of freelancing attracts a lot of fake gurus who love charging people for courses. Be wary of them and use the tips discussed earlier to figure out whether they're genuine. Keep in mind that most freelancing careers don't need a course of any kind. You can find all the information you need online. However, sometimes it might be worth joining a forum or a community where you can interact with likeminded people and have your questions answered.

Online Businesses

This is a huge area for you to potentially monetize. There's no end to the kind of businesses you can run online. It used to be that a blog was once considered the primary tool of online business. That's not the case anymore. These days you can run a successful online business using just an Instagram account or YouTube channel.

I must mention that if you're in debt, you should not focus on starting an online business. These businesses take time to bear fruit and they'll place a burden on your cash outflow. If you're carrying debt, all of your resources should be geared towards erasing it. Don't start an online business until you've erased your debt. Freelance for a while in order to raise additional cash but don't invest it elsewhere.

You can sell physical products or software. You can sell consulting services or sell courses. All successful online businesses have one thing in common: they operate in a specific niche. Even a huge news site such as Huffington Post has a niche. When you're starting out, you want to operate in as defined a niche as possible.

Take an inventory of all the things you're interested in and love talking about. What are your hobbies and interests? A good question to ask yourself is: Are you willing to talk about this topic for close to a year and make over 500 posts without anyone responding to you? If you are, then go ahead and start a blog or a channel on the topic.

If nothing appeals to you, you can choose to sell a physical product. This is essentially what dropshipping is. Pick a product that people are willing to spend money on and create an online store. You can use a service such as Shopify to create a store. This will cost you less than $29.99 per month.

You can locate a manufacturer using tools such as AliExpress or Oberlo. Once this is done, you'll need to drive traffic to your webpage using social media or paid ads. Alternatively, you could drive traffic to other people's websites using the same tools and embed your affiliate link. This will earn you commissions.

Describing the entire world of online business is out of scope for this book. However, here are some of the most popular business models out there that you can use:

- Blogging about a niche and monetizing using ads and affiliate links
- Creating a YouTube or social media channel and monetizing using affiliate links or directing people to your store/blog.
- Selling print on demand products - Websites such as Teespring allow you to upload your designs and sell them on t-shirts, mugs, bags and so on. Amazon also has a Merch by Amazon program that allows you to do the same.
- Selling eBooks - If you're knowledgeable about a topic you could write a book about it and sell it on Amazon or through your own website.
- Affiliate marketing using Pinterest and other social media. This allows you to sell products without a website. Embed your links in your profiles and direct traffic using that.

The key to making all of these models work is traffic. The problem is that generating interest and building traffic takes time. One way to shortcut your progress is to buy social media channels that already have inbuilt traffic. An Instagram account in the pets niche with 15,000 followers usually sells for $500-1,000. You can monetize this account or continue to build its reach and size. You can buy social media accounts at sites such as Fameswap, Social Tradia, and SWAPD.

Once you have enough engagement from your audience, you can sell them your product. Alternatively, you could charge brands for sponsored posts. If you can grow your account to 30,000 people, you can charge around $100 per post. You'll recover your investment within 10 posts.

If you post one sponsored post every week, you'll recover your initial investment in a little over two months. Everything after that is pure profit. This doesn't include the profit you can make selling your own product. If building an audience isn't your thing, consider taking this route. Just make sure you buy an account with real followers and real engagement and not fake ones with bots leaving comments.

Selling Courses

If you're knowledgeable about a particular topic, you can create a course on websites such as Udemy. This is a great way to generate passive income. You simply create the course once and then let it sell and bring you money in perpetuity. You can promote your course by having it reviewed by other websites and influencers in your niche.

Generally, online courses that sell well are priced around $40-$50. If 100 people buy your course, you've just made $4,000. Make sure you create great content that provides people with a ton of value. The word of mouth marketing alone will draw people towards you and you'll create a perpetual passive income stream.

If you're a good photographer then consider listing your photos on websites such as Shutterstock or Getty Images. These websites will pay you a small royalty every time someone uses your photo for promotional purposes. It isn't a huge money earner, but over time it adds up to give you a nice cash flow that is completely passive. You can expect to earn around $100 if you have a library of 500 photos.

This doesn't sound like much, but if you're an avid photographer it's not going to cost you too much time to upload these photos. It's not something you can make a living from but it's a decent income stream. Photography can also provide you with a good side hustle as a freelancer, so this is something you should consider if you're genuinely interested in it.

Language courses also do very well on Udemy. There really is no limit to the kind of courses you can create. The key is to drive traffic towards it. You can do with a social media platform, a blog, or influencer marketing. Influencer marketing is where you pay someone with a good sized account and have them recommend your product. You can leverage their audience size to your own benefit.

Etsy

Etsy is an extremely underrated way of making money online. This is because it's the one marketplace where you need to have actual skills and cannot outsource too many things. It's a great place for artists and craftspeople to sell their creations. If you're a photographer, consider selling digital prints or framed prints of your work through your own store.

All kinds of craftspeople can sell their wares on Etsy. Handmade jewelry, paintings, and other artwork all sell really well. Home decoration products have a huge audience on the website as well. If you have a knack for coming up with funny sayings, you can print them on a t-shirt and target people looking for them.

The key to Etsy success is once again traffic. The marketplace won't do much to promote your listing. However, through the use of intelligent influencer marketing and social media posts, you can drive traffic to your goods and build a steady revenue stream. Check out my friend Kevin Smith's book "Etsy Marketing" to learn more about this! You can find it on Amazon.

Local Gigs

Local businesses need help all the time and they typically don't advertise these openings. If you happen to live in a major city, working as a tour guide or conducting walking tours is a great way for you to earn extra cash. You could also work at the local museum or the local library.

Some companies hire delivery drivers. Local restaurants always need delivery help since this tends to add too much costs to their overhead and finding reliable people is hard. This is a great way to earn some cash with your vehicle on the side. Call your local pizza parlor and offer your services.

You'll even end up making a lot of money through tips. You can also check an app called Taskrabbit. This app has a listing of tasks that need to be fulfilled and pays a certain amount of money per task.

eBay Selling

Instead of merely selling your stuff on eBay, you can source items that typically sell well on the website and generate a profit for yourself. The best places to source great bargains are flea markets, garage sales, and estate sales. As morbid as it sounds, many eBay sellers frequent funerals and follow estate sales since this is where stuff tends to be priced really cheaply.

Make sure you conduct thorough research into what sells well on eBay and to document your fuel and transportation costs into your expenses.

Real Estate Investing

Real estate investing costs money and you can invest for a low price through the stock market. I'll talk about this later in this book. One method to make money through physical real estate is by becoming a real estate wholesaler. Wholesalers locate cheap or rundown properties and put sellers in touch with buyers.

In exchange for this they either take a finder's fee or they transfer the property to the buyer. For example, a wholesaler finds a property selling for $35,000. They sign the purchase agreement with the seller and assign the contract to the buyer for $50,000. The buyer is unaware of the purchase price paid and does not come into contact with the seller.

If you've ever seen signs that say "we buy ugly houses" you've just seen a real estate wholesaling tactic in action. These signs target sellers who have rundown properties and wish to sell quickly. Place a few signs around your neighborhood and tour the area to spot possible opportunities.

Network in your local real estate investment club and on websites such as Biggerpockets and you'll come in touch with home flippers. These people rehab homes and sell them for a profit. You can get their details and offer to bring them properties they might be interested in.

Some sellers will not want to talk to you unless you can show them proof of funds. A letter or a bank statement from your buyer will do the trick. Of course, you'll need to have a strong relationship with them for them to give you this. Bring them a good enough property and you'll be in business.

Another method is to approach the owner of a large property in your neighborhood and offer to execute what's called a master lease. This is where you run the building for them and manage the property. It takes a lot of time and you'll need to have a handyman on hand to address tenant concerns. However, you can charge and collect rent and pay the owner their cut of it while you keep the rest.

Master leases are attractive to owners of properties who are old and aren't interested in managing it day to day. Property management companies usually charge 10% of monthly rents and this might be too high for them. If you can find a 10 unit property where tenants pay $1000 per month, you can earn a steady $800 at the very least. You can earn more by increasing the rent or adding curb value to the property.

These options require a lot of work, but if you have the time then they make a lot of sense.

Daytrading, Cryptotrading, Forex Trading

At some point, everyone who wants to make money dabbles in these. It's entirely possible to make money through these methods but understand that the odds are stacked severely against you. The success rate of these methods has been estimated to be 10% (Godfrey, 2020). These are pretty dismal odds.

What's more, trading of any kind requires you to spend a lot of time in front of the screen and the payoff isn't always worth it. A good trader can generate 80% or more returns on their capital per year. However, if you have just $1,000 to trade, $800 per year isn't going to do much for you.

Given the huge interest, these activities attract a large number of fake gurus who claim to know all kinds of secrets that unlock the markets. FX especially has a lot of these people. From claiming fancy patterns to proprietary trading systems, it's easy to get scammed. Only sign up for advice from someone who provides you with professionally audited trading records that prove they make money from trading the markets.

If they claim to have worked for a hedge fund or even ran a hedge fund (which is highly unlikely), ask to see their securities dealer license. If they worked in a developed market such as the United States, the United Kingdom, or any other Western jurisdiction, they must have a license. If they claim to have worked in Cyprus or some unpronounceable country, they're most likely lying.

Just as with internet marketers, watch out for the signs of fraudulent behavior and you'll save yourself a lot of money.

Chapter 4:

Funding Your Goals and Dreams

Everyone has goals and dreams that they wish to fulfill. The trouble is that most people borrow money to make their way there. You see this all the time with real estate entrepreneurs. They borrow immense amounts of money and don't have clear exit strategies in place.

Their properties are mortgaged and yet they claim to own them and ascribe the value of those properties to their net worths. This is how a 20 year old claims to have a million dollar property empire. It just isn't true. Even worse the person claiming this in good faith is ultimately clueless as to how wrong things can go.

I'm not saying using debt to grow your business and net worth is bad. What's important for you to realize is that debt isn't the only way to fuel your growth. Utilizing high levels of debt cuts both ways. Let's use a hypothetical scenario to see how this works. Let's say you buy a house worth $100 and pay just $20 of your own money while $80 comes from the bank.

I'm going to ignore interest costs here since this is a simple scenario. If the value of the property rises by 10% to $110, you've earned a 50% return (since $10 is half of $20) on your money. A 10% increase has turned into 50% thanks to the power of debt. However, what if the property declines in value by 10% to $90? You've now lost 50% of your investment.

Debt can magnify your gains and losses. Most investors look at the gains and ignore the losses portion. This is what convinces them to buy a house with a mortgage and then live in it without monetizing the asset. If your property isn't producing cash flow that you can use, it isn't an asset. It's a massive liability.

What if someone gave you a brick and told you that you can keep the brick for the next 30 years as long as you pay the person $400 per month? Would you take this deal? You'd probably chuck the brick right back at them. Yet, this is what people do with their homes all the time and think of it as being an investment.

This is just one example of how people use debt to work their way towards their dreams due to ignorance. Banks and real estate developers convince you that debt is the only way forward. After all, the more you borrow, the more they earn so it's natural they'd say this.

In this chapter, you're going to learn how you can work your way towards your goals without assuming undue levels of risk. It's perfectly possible to own your home by the age of 40 or to have a million dollars in the bank by the time you're 55. It all depends on how well you define and then establish processes related to your goals.

Defining Your Goals

The first step is to define what sort of goals you want. Where do you want to live at a certain age (say 40)? What kind of a life will you be living? There aren't any easy answers to these questions. On the surface of it you might say "I want to live in a mansion with a billion dollars in my bank account" or something like that.

Wanting this is perfectly fine. However, is it what you truly want? Contrary to what you might think, money brings satisfaction only up to a certain point. A study conducted at Purdue University determined that the amount of money a person needs to earn every year before taxes for emotional wellbeing is between $60,000 to $75,000. In order for a person to be financially independent, they need to earn $95,000 (Martin, 2017).

That doesn't sound anything like the million dollar figures that are tossed around does it? Obviously, this applies to an individual and doesn't take into account familial expenses. However, if you and your partner earn money in this range, odds are that you'll be able to live very comfortable lives.

Feeling rich is far more important for our well-being than being rich. Instead of focusing on the amount of money you need, focus instead on the kind of lifestyle you desire. Do you wish to be location independent? Do you want to travel the world and live in places for a few months at a time and take it slow?

Or do you want to be someone who's running a company that makes a difference? Do you want to produce goods that make a difference to people's lives? Do you want to be location independent and still run a company? This is perfectly possible thanks to the power of the internet.

You can live for six months to a year at a time in Bali or some tropical paradise and run a company remotely with employees all around the world. The news will have you believe that the world is getting worse and more unstable but in reality, it's been getting more unlimited for awhile now. It depends on your perspective.

The question of what you truly want to do is tough to answer. The first reaction your mind will have when asked this question is to present a bunch of choices, all of which seem appealing. Choosing between them will seem tough and there's also the danger of picking something that just isn't a good fit for you.

Thankfully, there's a simple mental trick you can use to make this choice a lot easier.

Invert

This technique is used by the billionaire investor Charlie Munger. If you haven't heard of Munger, he's the vice chairman of Berkshire Hathaway. Still doesn't ring a bell? He's Warren Buffett's business partner and has been since the 1960s. Munger is older than Buffett and by all accounts has had to deal with more setbacks in his life.

To give you an idea of what he's had to deal with, he was broke, divorced, and lost his only child to leukemia at the age of 31. He was a trained lawyer but wasn't making much money at the time, and he lost an eye a few decades later when an operation was botched. All of these crises have given Munger a certain philosophy that he uses to approach life and money.

Inversion is a tactic he's repeatedly spoken about when asked about decision making. He uses it not only in his investment decisions but also in his daily life. The model is quite simple. In order to solve a problem, ask the opposite question of the problem and seek answers.

If you want to figure out what it is you want to do in your life, don't ask yourself "what do I want to do?" Instead, ask yourself "What do I not want to do?" The inverted question is usually a lot easier to answer because everyone knows what they don't want. This isn't a coincidence. It's how our brains are structured.

Our brains have an in-built negativity bias that draws our attention to the negatives in a situation far quicker than the positives. It's why fear based advertising is so powerful. Phrases like "Limited time only," "Only while stocks last," and "Don't get left behind" move us into action far more effectively than "Save 50%," "Stocks last till Tuesday," and "Gain x, y, and z benefits."

By inverting the question you're using that negative bias to help you. Once you come up with a list of all the things you don't want to happen in your life, simply avoid doing the things that lead to those results. For example, you don't want to be broke two decades from now.

What are the actions that lead to a person being broke? Not saving their money, not tracking their expenses, splurging on emotional buys all the time, not enforcing their discipline when spending, chasing after the latest shiny object, investing in things they don't understand, being impatient and falling for con artists, borrowing too much money to pay for their lifestyle... the list goes on and on.

Simply avoid doing all of these things and you'll automatically have money in the bank. It really is that simple. You've already seen how it's close to impossible to not become a millionaire if you dedicate a small amount of money to investing in an ETF in the stock market. It doesn't require special knowledge or any work that is beyond your abilities.

So ask yourself these inverted questions to arrive closer to the answer of what you really want to do. Inversion won't take you all the way to your perfect situation. However, it will eliminate all the situations you don't want to automatically align you with what you want to do. In this better frame of mind, you'll be able to focus and answer the non inverted question a lot better.

Here's another question that a lot of people ask themselves: "What makes me happy?" This is a huge question and is extremely tough to answer. Now ask yourself, "What makes me unhappy?" This is a lot easier to answer! Poor health, poor financial means, working mindlessly at something you detest and being in a terrible relationship would make you unhappy. That's really all there is to it.

Avoid all of these things and you'll be much happier. Once you're in that happier state, you can fine tune your life to increase your prosperity. It all begins by inverting the problem and then moving forward.

Creating a Roadmap

Once you've narrowed down your list of goals to a few points that will not make you miserable at the very least, it's time to create a basic roadmap of how you plan on getting there. These goals apply to your life so there's no end date to them. You can place a specific end date to these but if you don't have one in mind, it's perfectly fine.

When it comes to goal setting, it's important to specify how you'll know when you've gotten there. How will you feel or what will the physical evidence look like that confirms you've achieved what you wanted? Write these out. Once these are written, forget about them and start focusing instead on the process that will take you there.

This is where a lot of people get lost. They focus on the goal and on how it will feel and start daydreaming. The successful ones focus on the process while checking in with the ultimate goal now and then. They know they're on the path so what's the point of looking at the destination. If they focus on walking the path, they'll get there at some point.

Developing a process to achieve your goal is as simple as reverse engineering your goal's evidence. Let's say you want to have a million dollars in the bank by the age of 40. I'm going to assume you're 22 now. This gives you 18 years. One way of getting there is to invest in stocks as I mentioned earlier.

In order to reach a million in 18 years with zero principal right now, you'll need to invest $27,000 per year. This assumes an average return of eight percent per year, which is lower than the historic average. $27,000 per year is $2,250 per month. If you're earning $2,000 per month, this seems like a daunting figure.

$2,250 per month in savings is now your short term goal. Stop focusing on it and focus on creating a process that can bring you this amount in savings. Let's assume this represents 50% of your income. This means you'll need to make $4,500 every month. Another short term goal.

How can you make $4,500 per month? Your current active income is $2,000. Can you generate money from a side hustle such as freelance writing or English language teaching that will amount to $1,000? That brings you to $3,000 per month. Can you ask for a raise at work or find a better paying job that increases your salary to $2,500 per month? You're now at $3,500.

The additional $1,000 can be developed by investing in a business that you can automate. Perhaps you can buy an Instagram account or you can start a print on demand (POD) business. Let's use the example of a POD business. Your gross profit on every t-shirt will amount to $8. Assuming you use influencer marketing and have the products designed, you'll need to spend around $500. This means you need to sell 63 shirts to breakeven.

If you can sell 100 per influencer campaign, you'll earn a profit of $300. Run four campaigns a month, one per week, and you'll earn $1,200 in profit. Add this to your other income streams and you're now earning $4,700 per month.

You now have a framework of the things you need to implement. These are:

1. Asking for a raise or increasing your active income (salary).
2. Establishing a side hustle that brings $1,000 per month.

3. Establishing a business that passively brings $1,200 or so per month.

These three points have sub-processes that you need to execute. In order to ask for a raise, you need to document everything you do at work. You need to plan what you'll ask your boss. What will you do if they say no? How do you plan on finding alternative opportunities? Can you do this in parallel with planning to ask for a raise? Of course you can! Go on LinkedIn and start networking.

You want to find a side hustle income source that will pay you steadily. The money is what's important so you don't want to put yourself in a position where you're working and not getting paid. Contact agencies that can guarantee you a steady stream of work. If they cannot do this, stop working for them and find someone else. You're running a business and need to prioritize your time above all else.

In order to start a business you need to save some money. Plan how you'll do this with the income you currently have (not projected income). Even if you're just setting aside a few dollars per month, you're doing great. As your income rises, this contribution will increase. Meanwhile, research everything you can about the business. Be prepared so that when the time comes, you'll be ready to pull the trigger and execute.

Remember my previous points about what to do if you're carrying debt. You need to pay that off first. Create a debt repayment plan and do whatever it takes to destroy your debt. Adopt the attitude that it is your mortal enemy and you'll get rid of it soon.

Plan these processes out and focus on executing them as perfectly as possible. This is how a million dollars are made. It took nothing more than basic arithmetic and some common sense to figure out a plan. Do you still think you can't achieve this? If you still think so, refer to the final chapter regarding mindset.

How to Fund Your Dreams

Figuring out your goals and dreams is one thing. Understanding how you can fund them is entirely another. Most people use debt to fund their goals and this is just another way to decrease your financial wellbeing. Debt can be used to fuel your goals but you need to use it intelligently.

The fact is that if you're reading this book, you probably have a poor relationship with debt and are best served by staying away from it for now. Once you've increased your income and understand how much of a burden debt is, you'll be able to use it intelligently.

The following tips will help you get closer to your goals and will help you get there without having to resort to using debt.

Get Out of Debt First

Hopefully this message has sunk in by now but in case it hasn't: Get out of debt before doing anything else. Trying to build wealth while carrying debt is like driving a vehicle with the brakes still on. It's perfectly fine to build a roadmap that will take you to your dreams but in the present moment, focus on eliminating debt as much as you can.

Any additional income you earn must be diverted to your emergency fund and towards debt principal repayment, with the latter being the larger contribution. If you have the time, establish a side hustle that won't cost you any money and divert all of that income towards paying down your debt principal.

Principal payments are far more powerful than interest payments. Once you begin paying down your principal, your monthly payments will decrease because you owe less money. This in turn gives you more cash to pay your principal down. It's a virtuous cycle that will boost your cash flow slowly and steadily.

It will be tempting to aim to make $10,000 per month immediately and get rid of your debt in a fell swoop. You might even read a bunch of success stories that make these claims. However, these are most likely fraudulent. Even if they are true, such results are a function of luck and not of processes that can be replicated.

Processes are what make you money and keep you financially free. Invest your time into creating these and you'll see results. If you get lucky along the way it's a bonus.

Research and Reverse Engineer

Much like how I walked you through a sample roadmap in the previous section, you'll need to sit down and figure out your own roadmap. This is an exciting process since you're literally plotting your way to financial freedom. If you feel jaded or start thinking that these goals are not achievable, then recall a previous example I highlighted.

If I placed all the food you had to eat over a month a month in front of you, there's no way you'd get through all of it. When creating a roadmap, you're effectively looking at all the food you need to eat over the next 20 years or so. How could you possibly think you can get through all of it at once?

Feeling intimidated by your goals also happens to be a good thing. If you know how to achieve it, there's no need to plan for it. You need plans to figure out stuff you have no idea about. It's what pushes you outside your comfort zone and allows you to grow.

Reverse engineering is where you get to nail down the exact amount of money you need to achieve your goals. Take it slow with this step. If this is the first time you're doing this, you will make mistakes. This is fine. In addition to this, you'll find that some of your original estimates and plans will seem wildly optimistic or pessimistic.

This is a part of the learning process. Accurately estimating everything isn't the point of this exercise. What you want is to get moving and start working on your processes.

Timelines

Timelines can be problematic because they're easy to get wrong. We often underestimate what can be achieved in a decade and overestimate what can be done in a day. A goal that you wish to hit in six months might be perfectly realistic but it might seem daunting when viewed from the current position.

As I said previously, human beings are notoriously poor at forecasting. However, adding a timeline to your goals is a good way to motivate yourself. The key is to make the timeline a part of the end goal and not a part of the process. Don't set a timeline for your process execution.

Instead, aim to execute as much as you can, whenever you can. You will have good and bad days. Telling yourself that you will work 5 hours a day on your goals after you're done working at your job everyday is a nonsensical thing to aim for. What if you fall sick? Will you still work for this long?

People get carried away by entrepreneurs who tweet that they work 120 hours per week building their businesses. Some people wear it as a badge of pride. The truth is that while it might suit them, it might not suit you. Your primary objective should be to respect yourself.

Pushing yourself unnecessarily when your body and mind are not in a position to work is disrespecting yourself. If you're thinking this means you need to give in to laziness then you're wrong. If you're sufficiently motivated by your goals and if they mean enough to you, you'll figure out a way to work at executing the processes attached to them.

Fixing a certain number of hours to work does not help most people. Instead, tell yourself you'll get there in a certain number of years and let it go. In the present, execute everything you need to.

Discipline

Dreaming big is of no use unless you build a disciplined framework for yourself. As I mentioned earlier, discipline is what sets you free and it isn't a prison of any kind. At the root of your discipline is your ability to budget and track your spending. It all begins with this.

As long as you have a handle on your cash inflows and outflows, you'll be just fine. You won't have to worry about overspending or about not having enough money. Your budget will tie itself to your processes automatically. For example, if you've gotten rid of your debt and are looking to establish a passive business, you'll need to contribute money to it.

Your budget will help you figure out how much you can allocate. Do whatever it takes to track your spending and allocations and you'll find yourself moving closer to your goals. Reread the tips I gave you in the previous chapter about creating a budget and about tracking expenses until it sinks in fully.

In addition to a budget, create another spreadsheet that tracks your progress towards your goals. This will help motivate you and will make your goals seem much more real. If your goal is net worth related, calculate your net worth every month or every quarter and measure your progress.

Scale Well

When you first start out at the bottom, you're not going to have too much money to allocate to all of the things I mentioned in the previous chapter. The wrong thing to do is to get discouraged and feel you'll never get there. Instead, contribute whatever you can, even if it's a dollar. If you don't have a dollar, contribute a cent.

People's incomes might just about cover their debt expenses and leave very little for them to live. If you're in this situation, don't worry (although that's easier said than done). Instead, work to either increase your active job related income or find a side hustle that gives you steady work.

I'd like to emphasize the word "steady" in that phrase. For example, if you're a talented artist and are thinking of starting a side gig where you sell paintings, ask yourself whether this is a steady gig or not. Will you get a certain amount of money every month as close to guaranteed as possible?

When you're in debt and your expenses are greater than your income, you need to emphasize steadiness in the short term. If your paintings aren't going to sell consistently and if you cannot reliably ballpark the amount of money you'll receive from them, don't devote too much time to them.

It's far better for you to work a second job that pays you a steady amount of cash every month. Your paintings can be turned into a business once your debt is paid down. As of now, it's not reliable since it isn't a steady source of income. This applies no matter how much you love painting or feel it's your calling. Work on it in your free time but don't sacrifice the time you could potentially be earning money for it.

Most people get this wrong and end up creating even more frustration in their lives. If your paintings don't sell and if you can't find consistent buyers, you're only going to become more frustrated. If you're instead earning steady cash from two sources, your expenses are under control even if you aren't saving much.

Work on your paintings over the weekend or on one day of the week. If they sell, it's a nice bonus for you and you'll feel good about yourself. This will put you in a better frame of mind and you'll automatically make better decisions that will improve your life.

As your income increases, contribute more money towards your goals and the contribution line items I mentioned in the previous chapter. Remember which ones become active once debt is paid off and contribute accordingly.

Save Wisely

Saving gets a bad rap in personal investing circles. There is some merit to the arguments that are put forth. The reasoning is that saving merely helps you stay afloat. Investing helps you build wealth and stay ahead of the curve. However, your personal finance journey begins with saving.

As I mentioned in the previous chapter, you need to save enough money until you have an emergency fund equal to six months' living expenses saved up. Once this money is saved, you can choose to save an additional amount that you feel is enough to address any personal emergencies.

Saving money in a savings account or in a certificate of deposit above this amount is unwise. This is because you're effectively losing money. You're not losing cash but you are losing opportunities to grow your money by leaving it stagnant in an account. If you have this emergency cash built up and if your income streams are steady, you can afford to take some risks and invest it in the market or as a downpayment for a property.

Understanding the risk to reward ratio of various investment options available is important. For example, people often wonder whether a home or the stock market is a better investment. The answer is that it depends. For most people, a home is a good investment since it builds your net worth despite assuming debt.

To mitigate the debt, generate cash flow from the property. However, if you're able to earn a better return from stocks, don't buy your own home until you absolutely have to. For example, Warren Buffett earns much better returns in the stock market than in real estate. For this reason he owns just one property in his name, which is the home he bought back in the 1960s in Omaha, Nebraska. He bought it at the behest of his wife and paid $66,000.

So let go of absolute statements such as "this is better than that" and so on. In investing and saving money, it all depends on your rate of return and which option gives you the highest reward for the lease possible risk.

High Yield Savings

Before you can start investing you need to optimize your savings. Choose a high yield savings account that gives you instant access to your cash. A traditional savings account pays less than one percent these days but there are some online bank accounts that pay over one percent.

Technically, even this isn't a lot but it will build passive income for you. Another option is to build a CD ladder. I'll explain what this is in the chapter on investing.

One Time Windfalls

Everyone receives a windfall of cash now and then. You might win a sweepstakes or some other prize unexpectedly. What most people do is spend this money immediately on their wants. What you will do, because you're an intelligent person, is bank it.

The government occasionally hands out stimulus checks and every year you may receive a tax return check from the IRS. Instead of spending this money, you should immediately direct it towards making it work for you.

Money is meant to be deployed towards the things that make your life easier. It works best when it's put to work towards making sure your long term goals are met. This doesn't mean you should not spend it on short term wants. Allocate money towards entertainment and spend that money.

The rest needs to be put to work. Money serves you best when it's working to make you more money. Having it sitting in the account (over and above your emergency funds) is simply wasting it. It's like buying an ice cream and them watching it melt away.

Automate

A top tip to ensure you save money regularly is to automate the contributions towards your goals. Debt payments should also be automated assuming you have the cash to cover these payments. Once your savings and contributions are on autopilot, you won't have any problems saving money.

Some banks offer goal oriented savings accounts where you can allocate money towards a goal and earn interest on it. Create separate accounts and transfer money to them automatically when you receive your paycheck. Make sure you're not losing money on transfer fees. If your bank charges you money then consider cash withdrawals or simply create a spreadsheet that tracks the various amounts despite the money being in the same account.

This isn't technically automating anything but all it takes to maintain the account is for you to update the spreadsheet with the appropriate numbers.

Plan

To buy a property you'll probably need to save a significant amount of cash for your down payment. While most banks require you to put 20% down on the property value, understand that the higher your downpayment is the lower your monthly mortgage payment will be and the quicker you can own your property.

There are options available through the Federal Housing Authority (FHA) where you can put just three to 10% down, but you need to be debt free before doing this. A traditional mortgage also works much better for your investment goals if you're free of other forms of debt.

When it comes to mortgages, you'll need to pay the downpayment and closing costs. Closing costs can be three to four percent of the property's value. If the property is worth $100,000 you'll need to pay $4,000 for closing. In addition to this, if you pay less than 20% down you'll need to pay mortgage insurance every month.

This amount is typically included in the monthly payment so it's not a separate cash burden. However, you will pay more over the life of the loan compared to someone who has paid 20% or more down.

Is there an advantage to paying more than 20% down? It depends on what your goals are and what you can put the additional cash towards. For example, if you're earning a steady return in the stock market through a diversified portfolio then paying more than 20% doesn't make sense. If your passive business is giving you a good return then paying an additional amount isn't logical.

However, if you have no other investment related ventures, then reducing your debt burden will make sense. It makes even more sense if you can reduce your monthly cash payment to a level where the rent you earn from the property covers it entirely.

Calculating these numbers takes some time so make sure you use a mortgage payment calculator. Always generate cash flow from your property and don't let it sit there doing nothing. Many old time investors advice you to pay yourself and consider rental payments a waste.

This is a clouded view of how money works. As you've learned thus far in this book, it's all about which option works best for your money. You should invest accordingly and educate yourself with regards to the returns you can expect and how these tie in to your goals.

Needless to say you should do all of this once you're free of debt. If coming up with a downpayment is still an issue, you can check whether you qualify for any local or federal grants that can help you. Having someone else co-sign the loan for you is also an option.

Be Prepared

Regular financial advice will tell you to be prepared to seize the day. How does one seize the day though? It's done by preparation. You never know when opportunity will come calling, and when it does you want to have cash on hand that's ready to be deployed and grown.

In order to seize these opportunities, you need to have established processes that make sure you have the cash on hand. If one happens to come by and if you don't have the cash yet, don't worry about it. If you missed it due to not having processes in place, this is something to worry about.

As long as you're working towards establishing the structure I outlined in the previous chapter, you'll find that opportunities will always make themselves known to you. Opportunity doesn't knock just once or twice. The world is a pretty abundant place and it keeps coming around.

Your job is to be prepared and have the cash on hand to invest in opportunities; keep preparing and wait patiently. Something will come up and you'll be in a position to cash in and boost your wealth.

If you've loved what you've read so far, please let me know what you think by leaving a honest review for this book online. I'd really appreciate it!

Chapter 5:

Taking Your First Steps to Save

Cash

People in college lack financial discipline for the most part. This is perfectly fine. After all, no one has ever taught them the value of financial discipline at that age. However, as you grow older it's important to maintain and build retirement related goals as described in the previous chapter.

Without these goals in place you won't have any idea of how well you're doing or what your financial situation looks like. Saving money can seem like a tough task when your income is low and if your debt is overwhelming. This chapter is going to help you create a plan that will allow you to start saving.

It all begins with defining your goals. This process has already been described in the previous chapter. If you still have doubts about how it works or haven't defined your goals yet, read that section once again and put the advice into action. Once you've done this, everything becomes a lot easier.

You'll find that when you reverse engineer how much you need to save, you'll be able to allocate certain amounts of money towards your goals and debt payment. Your goals will clarify your priorities as well. For example, if you have high levels of credit card or student loan debt, erasing this should be your number one priority.

If you're free of debt then congratulate yourself! You're already ahead of the large majority of Americans. From this point on, it's just a matter of following some tips and general principles.

Getting Started With Retirement

Retirement seems a long way away when you're in your 20s. Retirement comes in many shapes and sizes. The traditional definition of it is to stop working at a job and then sit around and do nothing. The fact is that this kind of retirement doesn't suit most people.

Sitting around doing nothing only results in your brain decaying since there's nothing stimulating it anymore. Most people would not want to live this kind of a life when presented the choice as a long term option. So how should retirement be defined?

Perhaps a better way of defining it is to say that retirement is when you're financially free and don't need to work in order to support yourself. You're free to choose whether you wish to work or not. This is a far more positive definition of retirement since it emphasizes the freedom it brings.

It also decouples retirement from having anything to do with age. Technically speaking Mark Zuckerberg retired when he was 22 years old. He was well on his way to becoming a billionaire and had already made enough money to last him two lifetimes. Hitting this state of being is what everyone wants.

Yet everyone plans to "retire" when they're 65. Instead of adopting the default option, why not set a target for when you wish to be financially free and then reverse engineer your life from that? It'll help you figure out what your income needs to look like and what you need to do in order to get there.

Calculate

The first step to take is to calculate. A retirement calculator such as the one at **https://smartasset.com/retirement/retirement-calculator** will help you figure out how much you need. The best part about this calculator is that it takes the cost of living into account as well.

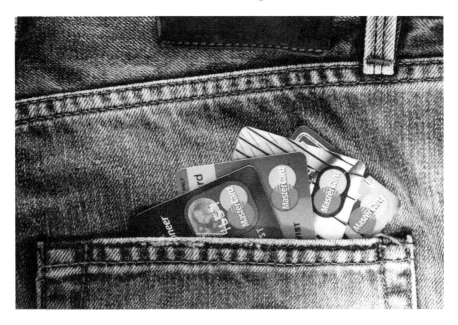

Most retirement calculations don't take the cost of living into account. What happens is that once people retire at the age of 60 or 65, they find that their fixed income is less than what they were making through their salary. The result is that they need to adjust to living in conditions that are worse than what they were used to.

When using the calculator above, the key input is the cost of living expenses. You can enter pretty much any amount you want but ask yourself whether you can truly live in that location for the amount you entered. For example, you can enter an amount of $2,000 to live in San Francisco. However, only a madman would think you can actually live well with this amount in that city.

Calculating your retirement fund using that calculator also assumes you'll be retiring at the traditional age. It helps to use this in calculations since it can work as a minimum threshold for your retirement.

What I mean is that if you know you're setting aside this amount every month into an account then you're guaranteeing retirement at a certain age. Whatever you contribute over and above this is a bonus for you and brings retirement that much closer. The calculator mentioned above assumes you'll live till you're 95 so it's quite conservative.

Of course, with medical advances increasing, it's possible human beings will break the 100 barrier with increasing frequency in the coming decades. Either way, use this calculator to figure out what your minimum contribution must be in order to guarantee retirement around 60-65 years of age.

Much like reducing expenses, this is a conservative way of looking at retirement. However, it works because it enforces basic discipline. You'll be surprised at how little you need to set aside in order to have your money last through retirement. If you plan on living on $2,000 every month, all you need to allocate in order to retire at 60 is $303 per month.

This is $10 per day and is a sum that anyone can set aside as savings.

Understand Compounding

Compounding is something I've mentioned briefly earlier in this book. It's possible that you didn't quite understand how powerful it is. To put it in short, compounding is one of the miracles of this world in terms of the power it has to build your wealth. It's something that every rich person does.

The best part about compounding is that it works for you for free. All it asks is that you don't disturb it and leave it be. Compounding effects can be seen everywhere, even outside the world of money. You learned about how developing processes and executing them are far more important than focusing on your goals.

This is just compounding in action. Consistent action that you take towards your goals will lead to results that are far greater than the sum of their parts. Compounding allows you to turn 1+1 into 11 instead of two. In order to be consistent with your compounding efforts, you need to do the same thing over and over again.

This means you need to invest a minimum amount every month over and over and let your savings or investment instrument takeover and do its thing. This is why long term investment pays out far more than short term trading. Traders can make a lot of money but they erect significant barriers to their success.

They increase their transaction costs in the markets by jumping in and out. They increase their tax burden thanks to attracting short term capital gains taxes. Most importantly, trading requires the practitioner to be able to predict the short term direction of the market accurately.

Doing this over and over again is unimaginably tough. This is why a very small percentage of traders are successful in the markets. The majority of people burn out and turn to long term investing since it's far less hassle to let your money sit there and grow. An investment that pays 10% every year will earn 10% whether the amount invested is $1 or $10,000.

The amount by which these investments will grow is different. However, thanks to the rate remaining the same, money keeps growing all by itself. If you were to plot a curve of how your money grows you'll find that it's exponential. An exponential curve starts off shallow but then quickly becomes steeper.

This is because the growth rate at first is small but as time goes on and as the amounts earned automatically increase, the amount invested grows faster. A good example of the power of compounding is Warren Buffett's net worth.

He became a billionaire at the age of 53. It took him almost 20 years to go from a million to a billion. He became a millionaire when he shut his investment partnership at the age of 35 or so. He became one of the richest men in the world by the age of 65 and has remained in the top five ever since.

Once he broke into the top five, his net worth has always hovered north of $60 billion. So it took him around a decade to go from a billionaire to one of the richest billionaires in the world. Contrast this with the time it took him to go from a million to a billion. This illustrates how compounding works and how your wealth grows in an exponential fashion when you sit back and let it work for you.

This is why Buffett has said he'll never sell his investments. Selling would halt his compounding in that investment and this hurts his long term appreciation. You should adopt the same approach.

Fix a Goal

You've learned about establishing a minimum contribution that will ensure you can retire by the age of 60-65. You know that you need to let your money compound and that you should not interfere with this at any costs. The question now is, when do you wish to become financially independent?

This is another question that can intimidate people and it brings all kinds of complexes to the fore. Your first reaction might be to say "right now." This is a bit unrealistic if you're reading a book like this. You will become financially independent by reading this book. However, unless you have a long lost rich relative. you're unlikely to reach there right now.

A good way to address this question is to use inversion. Ask yourself whether you want to live a financially independent life at the age of 40. How about 50? Play around with the numbers and match this to the answers you came up with when defining your goals and the kind of life you wish to lead previously.

You'll arrive at a certain number and you can reverse engineer how you can get there. The first question is to figure out how much money you'll need to live. Estimate this using the average living expense you'd expect to incur living this life. Don't worry about it being too expensive or out of reach.

The point is to dream at this stage. Remember you're terrible at forecasting so don't burden yourself with your miserable forecasting abilities. Instead, fix a goal and work backwards to create a roadmap. You've already learned how to do this.

Focus on executing your processes and you'll get there with a high degree of probability.

Use Retirement Accounts

The great thing about living in America is that, amongst other things, you can invest your money in retirement accounts. There are three types of accounts you can utilize. These are a traditional IRA, a Roth IRA, and a 401(k). The traditional IRA is the simplest retirement account.

You can allocate money towards that account from your pretax income. You'll be taxed on the basis of ordinary income when you withdraw your earnings at the age of 60. Prior to that you won't pay any taxes. There are contribution limits to an IRA so make sure you check that you maximize these limits. The contributions you make to an IRA can be deducted at tax time so this gives you a double whammy of saving plus reducing your expenses.

The Roth IRA can be contributed to after taxes have been deducted from your income. The great thing about a Roth is that you don't pay taxes on withdrawals. You've already paid your share of taxes so it's a great way to earn tax free income. Again, there are contribution limits but maximize this as much as possible. Roth contributions are not tax deductible.

A 401(k) is offered by employers and they're the same as traditional IRAs except for one feature: Matching. If your employer offers this feature, they'll match the amount of money you place in your 401(k). If you contribute $5,000, they'll contribute $5,000 as well. This is literally free money that your employer gives you.

Your aim should be to maximize this matching. If your boss sits you down and tells you to take it easy with your contribution, you're doing it right. If someone is offering you free money then why wouldn't you take it and put it to good use? Take full advantage of your employer's offer while you can since you know they won't hesitate to cut you loose if things go bad for them.

Most employers have maximum limits on matched contributions. If you can contribute right up to this limit, you'll double your wealth in no time. Imagine contributing $2,000 every month. Within a year, you'll have amassed $36,000 in principal in your 401(k) if your employer matches 50% of whatever you put into it.

A 401(k) is taxed the same way as a regular IRA is. You'll be taxed upon withdrawal after the age of 60. Look at it as a safe retirement account that keeps compounding over time. You'll learn what the best investment options are for these accounts shortly.

Roth IRAs can be used to minimize taxes and eliminate them. However, there is a limit to how much you can contribute to these accounts. The good news is that you won't pay any taxes on either capital gains or on dividend distributions. If you don't know what either of those are don't worry, you soon will.

Taxes happen to eat up a significant portion of your gains in the stock market and minimizing them is the key to keeping a lot of your money. You cannot avoid taxes completely, but holding onto your investments for as long as possible and using retirement accounts intelligently is a great way to reduce their impact on your returns.

Aside from reading this book, take the time to educate yourself with regards to how they work. Smart investing is a part of good personal finance habits. You don't need to be a genius and invest in the best performing stock all the time. The beauty of investment is that if you hit even average returns, your money grows exponentially.

Build an Emergency Fund

I've mentioned this previously and I'll say it again. Before you think about investing in the markets you need to have an emergency fund in place. You should have at least six months' worth of expenses saved as cash. This cash should be accessible easily through a savings or liquid deposit account such as a certificate of deposit.

The emergency fund will grow in size as your income grows. This is because most people will increase their living expenses as they become more wealthy. Of course, your expenses should not increase at the same rate as your income. That's just being careless. However, don't go the other way and try to live like a pauper despite making a good amount of money.

Your money should provide you with the highest level of utility. Utility is an economic concept that can roughly be translated to "use" or "pleasure." Think of it as what you receive in return for using something. Money can bring you the things you want and pay for the things you need.

It can also multiply and grow all by itself provided you stay out of the way and let it do its thing. Your emergency fund gives you the security to do all of this. Without an emergency fund, you might find yourself withdrawing your investment capital to pay for expenses and this will stop your compounding.

The emergency fund also allows you to take a few risks with your money on business ventures that you might not be fully sure of. Business income can be up and down so it helps to have a backup in the form of a steady source of income and an emergency fund. This is why I mentioned previously that you should establish a side hustle that gives you guaranteed cash flow before launching a business.

This way you won't be in a position where your business "has" to make you money. You can execute your process optimally without worrying about whether you'll make enough to pay the bills.

Keep it Liquid

I mentioned above that your emergency fund must be in a liquid cash account. Liquid or liquidity refers to easily accessible cash that you can withdraw immediately. For example, funds held in a brokerage account are not liquid. You need to sell your investments and then wait for your broker to transfer the cash to your account.

In contrast, a savings account is a liquid source of cash. The cash always sits there and gathers interest. A certificate of deposit (CD) isn't as liquid as a savings account but it's far more liquid than other options. CDs are interest bearing instruments that you can buy from your bank.

They have a term associated with them that can run from a few months to a few years. At the end of the term you receive your deposit back along with the accrued interest. They generally pay slightly higher interest rates than savings accounts. The reason they aren't as liquid is because you'll pay a fee if you decide to withdraw your money before the term ends.

While a savings account won't give you the highest rate of return, it makes sense to park your money there and let it earn whatever interest it can earn. The longer you leave it dormant, the more it compounds. Be careful of savings accounts that require minimum balance deposits. High yield accounts typically have this requirement.

Choose accounts that require somewhere around $3,000 as minimum balances. Your six months' worth of living expenses will likely be greater than this amount and you can earn higher interest rates. Some banks pay interest on savings accounts and allow you to use them as checking accounts as well.

These accounts usually have withdrawal limits attached to them and won't pay you interest if you withdraw more than a few times. Make sure you read all the terms and conditions before signing up. Above all else, you don't want to sign up for an account that limits access to your money. That defeats the purpose of having a liquid cash account.

There should also be no monthly usage fees attached to the account. It costs the banks nothing to pay you interest so charging you fees makes no sense. Irrespective of the interest they pay you, don't sign up for such accounts.

There is a type of savings account that is offered by some banks where the more you invest, the more interest you earn. You can sign up for these accounts but take care to note the withdrawal limits and balance requirements. If there's a limit or penalty for withdrawing your own money, don't go anywhere near them.

Habits That Boost Saving

Like with reducing expenses there are some habits that will boost your ability to save. Engaging in these habits is quite straightforward and doesn't need special willpower or knowledge. They simply require awareness and the desire to improve your financial wellbeing.

Consistency

Consistency is what drives compounding. You've already learned how this works and also why compounding is so important for your financial security. A good way to approach saving is to adopt a minimum contribution method. This means you'll contribute a minimum amount to your savings account every month.

This kind of consistency applies not just to your emergency fund contributions but also to your other contribution accounts. Always divert a minimum amount of your funds to these accounts and let them grow. This way you'll be able to strike and take advantage when opportunity arises.

Don't worry if you can't contribute too much at this point in time. The amount of your contributions don't matter. The act of contributing is what matters the most. The actions you'll need to take to contribute a single penny versus $5,000 is exactly the same. If you're using separate accounts, you'll need to transfer this money. If you're using a single account and partitioning it on a spreadsheet, you'll need to update the numbers.

Get into the habit of managing your money, no matter how small it seems to you, and you'll find yourself having to manage more of it.

Don't Wait

People often tell themselves they'll start after some event happens or after something else is paid for and so on. Then there's the worst excuse of all: "I'll start tomorrow." There is no need to wait when it comes to saving and building your financial future. The only exception to this rule is if you wish to get started investing your money in the stock markets or in real estate ventures.

In those cases, it makes sense to go in with a certain minimum investment amount to get the most bang for your buck. In the case of real estate you can't play unless you have a minimum amount anyway. However, in every other case, such as building an emergency/financial freedom fund or a side business fund, there's no reason to wait.

As I said earlier, you never know when opportunity will arrive. You need to be ready and armed with cash to take advantage of it when it arrives. If your mind is telling you to wait or to postpone certain actions, this is just your old self trying to draw yourself back into the past.

It's trying to keep you in a place where your finances are uncertain and you have no clue where your money is going or how to make more. There are some really simple actions you can take right now to get started. First, figure out your goals as described previously. Second, reverse engineer them and figure out how much money you need.

Third, plan your process of increasing your current active income and start building your network in case you need to find another job. You're building leverage over your current employer by doing this so it's doubly beneficial. Resolve to do a little everyday. Transfer every dollar or penny into your reserve fund that you can. Congratulate yourself for taking action and build consistency over time by repeating these actions.

You'll soon establish a groove for yourself that will make behaving in this way become second nature for you.

Talk it Out

If you have a spouse or a long term partner, make sure you include them in your discussions about your financial future. I'll talk more about this in a later chapter, but for now understand that the two of you taking these steps together sets you both up for a greater level of success.

Keep Cash in an Account

This might sound like obvious advice but there are people out there who believe in holding onto cash in their homes. The idea is that if the apocalypse arrives and if banks meltdown, they'll have some resources left. If the worst does happen and if the economic system does crumble, why would cash have any monetary value?

Therefore, you should put your cash in an account. You can earn interest and put it to work. Another reason is that cash lying on hand is subject to inflation. Inflation is an economic concept that most people misunderstand. It's usually presented as something bad. However, a healthy economy has controlled levels of inflation. It indicates that the amount of goods and services within it is growing.

This is what causes prices to increase over time. A dollar today buys more than what it will 50 years from now. Inflation in the United States is at three percent annually. This means your dollar loses three cents of purchasing power every year. If you're following along, you'll also realize that a savings account does not give you enough money to even cover inflation.

Inflation is why you should invest in a side business or in the stock market. It's how your money will grow over time and you'll build real wealth. Those dollar bills in your hand today might feel good but they ultimately don't mean much. If you are so concerned about the apocalypse, buy physical gold and silver and store them in a vault. They'll be of much more use when zombies are among us than paper money.

Another thing I'd like to point out is that in the future, the rate of inflation will increase thanks to the economic policies that Western governments are following. Every time there's an economic crisis the government prints more money. This is the governmental equivalent of kicking the can down the road. Instead of taking action to fix issues today, they say they'll deal with it later.

Printing notes gives people easier access to money and credit in the short term, but in the long run it makes everything more expensive. It's simple supply and demand really. The more of something that exists, the less it costs if demand remains the same. The demand for money is the same but the supply has increased massively. This means the money is worth less.

While the number on the bill stays the same, it buys less stuff so inflation increases. U.S. inflation is unlikely to hit the levels experienced by countries such as Venezuela or Zimbabwe, but it will increase nonetheless. This makes investing your money and putting it to work more important now than ever.

Chapter 6:

How to Invest in Your 20s and 30s

When it comes to investing the mantra is simple: Start as early as you can. The best time to begin investing would have been when you were a twinkle in your parents' eyes. The second best time is right now. If you have five dollars sitting around in your pocket doing nothing, invest it somewhere so that it starts working for you.

Many people confuse saving with investing. They're not the same thing at all. Saving is a necessity because you need access to liquid cash. Investing is putting your money to work with the aim of having it return larger amounts of money. In other words, it's a profit driven enterprise and isn't defensive like saving is.

Investing is what brings you financial freedom in the largest means possible. When you invest your money, you're creating an asset. Assets are also a heavily misunderstood thing. Most people think purchasing a home via a mortgage and then living in it without generating cash flow is an asset.

This is the exact opposite of an asset. It's a liability. Anything that doesn't make you money is a liability. Take a moment right now and look around you. How many assets do you have and how many liabilities do you have? Now consider the possessions or environment of the average wealthy person.

They probably have a fancy watch. Watches, especially the high end Rolex kind, hold their value very well. They beat inflation and even appreciate in value. They're an asset. They probably wear plain clothes. Look at how Bill Gates or Jeff Bezos dress in everyday life. They're not blinging it out by any means. Clothes don't make you money unless you happen to be a celebrity.

Celebrities attract a lot of attention for the gear they wear to award ceremonies. Do you know that they're paid to wear these things? That fancy gown the Hollywood starlet wears on the red carpet is worn just once and is then sold to someone who wants to look like her. The celebrity wears it for free or might even earn a fee for generating publicity. It's the same with male celebrities and their watches or jewelry.

Next, let's talk about cars and modes of transportation. Not every wealthy person has fancy cars. Some of them collect cars but that's because they can indulge themselves in their hobbies. You don't see too many of them driving Rolls Royces or Ferraris. However, almost every wealthy person who can afford one owns a private jet.

Why is this? It's because the jet makes them money. First, the jet can be chartered to private companies and they earn fees with it. However, the bigger reason the rich own jets is because it saves them time and it allows them to make more money in that time.

Amazon earns billions of dollars in profit every year. Jeff Bezos' time is worth roughly a million dollars per hour. Why would he waste it standing around waiting for a TSA agent to prod him? Thus, the jet is one of the biggest assets a wealthy person owns despite being the most derided. Even Warren Buffett, who's noted to be thrifty, bought one for his company (christened "The Indefensible"). Fancy yachts work the same way, albeit to a lesser extent.

My point isn't to tell you to go out and buy a jet. Instead, it's to tell you to evaluate your possessions and your time from an asset/liability perspective. If your current fancy car is absolutely essential for you to complete your work, it's an asset. If you can complete your work with a cheaper car and if it isn't making you money, it's a liability.

The mortgaged property is an asset if it brings in cash and reduces your debt burden. If all you're doing is living in it, you're effectively paying the bank your rent instead of a landlord. Intelligent investing all comes down to understanding assets versus liabilities.

Another key point on which you must evaluate investments is opportunity cost. This sounds like a big term but is actually quite simple. Let's say you walk into a bakery and have enough cash to buy either a chocolate cake or a piece of artisan bread. You happen to like both but can choose just one. Which one should you pick?

If you pick the cake, you'll lose the chance to eat the bread and vice versa. Your decision ultimately comes down to which choice gives you the higher utility. However, each of these choices has a cost. As long as the utility of your choice is greater than the cost of losing the other choice, you're making a good decision.

If the satisfaction of eating the bread overcomes the pain of not eating the cake, you're making a good choice. What if the thought of losing either choice is higher than the pleasure a single choice will give you? In that case, go make some more money and buy both choices.

Evaluating your investment options in this way will make it clear which ones you ought to pursue. In monetary terms, the pain of losing a choice is simply the return your money would have earned by investing in it. For example, if you have a stock investment that can bring you 10% per year or a side business investment that can bring you 20% per year, you should obviously choose the latter.

However, you also need to take the investment needed into account. Physical real estate costs a lot more than a stock purchase but it puts real property into your hands. Thus, if you're looking to invest a large sum of money, the physical ownership part might override any return calculation from your investment choices.

This cost of giving something up is called opportunity cost in economic terms. Nothing is free since you're always having to give something up. As long as you're gaining more than you're giving up, you'll do well. With these basics in mind, let's look at the investment options available to you in your 20s and 30s.

Opportunities

There are two broad choices you have when it comes to investing: the stock market and physical real estate. Both have their pros and cons. Opportunity costs are what should drive your decisions. If anyone makes a blanket statement such as "This is better than that," they're speaking from their own perspective and it isn't a fact.

Let's look at the opportunities that exist in the financial markets first.

Certificates of Deposit

Technically, these are provided by your bank and you don't need to open a brokerage account to buy these. A CD, as I explained before, pays you a certain interest rate over a fixed term. They're a step above savings accounts in terms of liquidity but are just as safe. They typically pay a higher interest rate than savings accounts.

The best way to automate investing in CDs is to build what is called a CD ladder. Here's how you build one. Divide the money you want to invest into five portions. Invest each portion into a CD that expires in one, two, three, four, and five years' time.

At the end of the first year, once you receive your principal and interest back from the one year CD, reinvest that into a five year CD. Do this for every CD that expires and you'll always have a CD structure in place ranging from one to five years. Obviously, you should do this with money that you don't immediately need.

If your job situation is secure and if you're making enough income then you can invest half of your emergency fund in a ladder. This is because breaking the CD before the term ends will result in penalties and you'll lose the interest payment as well.

You don't have to have a CD ladder in place. However, if you're unsure of other options it's best to have it since your money will be working to some extent at the very least.

Stocks

Stocks are the most prevalent assets in the average investor's portfolio. They also happen to be extremely risky. A block of stock or a single share is literally a piece of a business. If you buy a share of Amazon, you're buying a piece of Amazon's assets and earnings. Most people unfortunately look at stocks as a casino game and play accordingly. It's no surprise that they end up losing their money.

Investing in individual stocks for the average investor is quite risky. This is because the average investor doesn't have a lot of time on their hands to properly evaluate the investment opportunity in front of them. Think of it this way. If your friend asked you to invest in their lemonade stand business, would you simply give them the money? Or would you take the time to understand what their business is about and how much money they truly make?

An alternative example is when someone asks you to buy one pair of shoes over another. Do you simply go ahead and buy what they ask you to or do you evaluate your choices? If you know nothing about shoes, would you simply walk in and buy whatever you're asked to buy by the salesperson? You'd conduct research or go with someone who knows a thing or two about shoes instead.

However, when it comes to stocks, everyone's an expert in analyzing companies. What makes you think you can understand the business of Amazon solely based on whatever Jeff Bezos says? Amazon is a huge company and it has multiple revenue streams. It's a complex business that requires time and effort to understand.

This is why if you don't have the time or the inclination to sit down and unravel a business' strengths and weaknesses, you should not invest in individual stocks. It's far too risky for you since you'll be investing in something you don't understand. It's far better to invest instead in funds.

I'll address funds shortly. If you do have the time and interest to analyze companies' business models, your first stop should be to read their 10-K filings. These are annual filings that companies file with the Securities and Exchange Commission (SEC) which regulates the markets. You'll find all information about their business, risks, and finances in these documents.

You should only consider investing in a company if you can understand what these documents convey. If you can't understand them, select a fund to invest in.

Bonds

Along with stocks, bonds are the other pillar of the financial markets. Both stocks and bonds help companies raise money for themselves. If a company needs to raise cash it can either sell shares of itself (pieces of itself) to the public or it can borrow money from them much like how you can borrow money from a bank.

The company does this by issuing bonds. You purchase the bond at what's called the face value and receive an interest payment over a fixed term. Bonds can have terms as short as a year or as long as 30 years or more. It's entirely up to the company that issues them.

At the end of the term, you'll receive the face value back. Much like stocks, bonds sell for different prices in the market. You can buy a bond at face value from the company and then resell it to someone else for a different price. Bond prices are quoted in percentages. If you see a bond being priced at 70, this means it's selling for 70% of its face value.

There are different grades of bonds and these grades are determined by their rating. The rating is provided by agencies such as Moody's and Standard & Poor's. While the individual rating labels vary, a rating of A and above indicates a safe bond that is likely to result in the investor receiving their principal/face value back at the end of the term.

The lower a bond's rating is, the higher its interest rate is. Investment grade bonds usually pay around five percent on their face value. They also sell for greater than their face value in the market. This reduces the yield on them. The yield is your return on investment and in a bond's case, it's calculated by dividing the interest payment by the price you pay for it.

If you pay $1,000 for a bond and receive a $50 payment every year, your yield is five percent. Thanks to being traded in the markets, a bond's face value and price will be different. This means the interest rate (called the coupon) and the yield will be different as well.

It might be tempting to chase high yields but these bonds lack safety. Investment grade bonds are usually secured by the company's property. This is not the case with lower grade junk bonds. They can be defaulted on without the company incurring major consequences. Companies often issue different grades of bonds so make sure you thoroughly research the characteristics of the bond before buying one.

Bonds have always been presented as being safer but this isn't true. A bond can fail and go to zero just as a stock can. It's just that bonds provide cash flow whereas a stock doesn't guarantee this. Stocks can provide cash flow if they pay dividends. The dividend yield on a stock (dividend payment divided by the price you pay) is typically two to three percent.

You can buy bonds on the cheap and hope their prices increase. However, this is just as risky as buying stocks. You'll still need to evaluate the prospects of the company and unless you have the time to do this, investing in individual bonds is also too risky. There are different kinds of bonds you can invest in:

- Corporate bonds.
- Municipal bonds or Munis - These are bonds issued by municipalities. They're free from local taxes but not from federal taxes.
- Treasury Inflation Protected Securities or TIPS - These keep pace with inflation but don't pay any interest. Your principal simply grows to keep pace with inflation.
- T Bills - These are short term bonds of less than a year issued by the U.S Government. You'll receive the face value along with accrued interest back at the end of the term.
- T Notes - These are government issued bonds that run for up to 10 years.
- T Bonds - These bonds are issued by the government and have maturities greater than 30 years.
- International corporate bonds.

You can invest in all of these individually but it's far better to invest in them using a fund.

Funds

I've been talking funds up quite a bit for the investor who doesn't have too much time on their hands so what are they all about? There is some diversity in the field of funds. Specifically, you can invest in the following:

- Mutual funds
  - Regular mutual funds
  - No load mutual funds
  - Index funds
- Exchange traded funds

Mutual funds have been around for a long time and have been the preferred choice of investment for many investors. However, they aren't always the best choice. The first thing to understand about a mutual fund is that it needs to stick to its investment objective rigorously.

The investment objectives of a fund can vary. There are mutual funds specialize in investing in small cap European stocks in the food industry for example. There really is no limit to the investment objectives a fund can set for itself. As an investor, such precise definitions of objectives allow you to capture that portion of the market's performance within your portfolio.

Every mutual fund has a manager whose objective it is to outperform what is called their benchmark. A benchmark is usually an index. An index is a collection of stocks that satisfy a certain criteria. For example, in the case of our European small cap mutual fund, the benchmark index would be one that tracks the movement of all European small cap stocks. As long as the value of the mutual fund rises to a greater extent than that of the benchmark, the manager is performing well.

Market outperformance of this kind is tough to capture. The mutual fund manager has plenty of time on their hands to analyze the market but this isn't easy. The average mutual fund underperforms the broad market, even if it outperforms its benchmark. For example, European small caps could increase by five percent but the overall market could rise by 10%.

This means you would have been better off investing in the broad market and not in one particular sector. The other problematic aspect with mutual funds is that their managers charge performance fees and other asset related fees. Some funds charge what is called an entry load fee. This is usually a percentage of the amount you invest in them.

There are also exit load fees where you're charged another percentage of your principal when you withdraw your funds. Lastly, there are performance fees which the manager charges even if they make a tiny amount of money and underperform their benchmark.

All of this results in a money transfer from the investor to the fund manager. It is possible to invest in mutual funds that outperform the market, but the average mutual fund happens to be a losing proposition.

To address this, the index mutual fund or index fund was created. While mutual funds seek to outperform their benchmarks, index funds merely capture their performance. They do this by buying all of the stocks in the benchmark. As a result, their performance is exactly the same as the index. In return, index funds charge a single management fee that is far less than the average mutual fund's fees.

Mutual fund fees can work out to between three to four percent of your capital per year. Index funds charge just 0.5% or less. Some index funds charge as little as 0.02%. The trade-off is that you'll capture just market average performance and will not outperform it.

However, this isn't so bad. If you had bought an index fund that tracked the entire stock market, you would have earned a 10% return every year on average. That's a pretty high rate of return. Compare this to the one or two percent a government bond yields and the sub one percent return savings accounts provide.

This return can make you a millionaire in 20 years as I've illustrated previously. When it comes to investing in stocks, targeting the average is a winning strategy. All you need to do is buy an index fund and sit back. You can invest in index funds that track dividend paying stocks, the entire stock market, tech stocks, stocks that have regularly increased their dividend payouts and so on.

You can also invest in index funds that track the real estate market and real estate investment trusts. I'll explain these shortly. The downside of an index fund is that they usually have high investment minimums. The typical index fund requires a minimum investment of $3,000.

To mitigate this, exchange traded funds or ETFs were launched. An ETF works the same way as a mutual fund does except its price fluctuates just like a stock's price does. Mutual fund prices are set before the market opens and you can buy and sell them only at that price. ETFs can have a vast number of strategies, just like mutual funds. A subset of them track indexes like index funds do. These don't have minimum investment requirements and have low fees as well.

Investing in index funds and ETFs is the safest option for a beginner without too much time to dedicate to analyzing individual companies to invest. They reduce your downside risk over the long run considerably because indexes are designed to go up in the long run.

The only scenario where your ETF investment will completely fail is if the American economy collapses. This is unlikely to happen despite what the financial news will have you believe. If you are concerned about this happening, you can invest in an ETF that gives you exposure to foreign stocks and economies.

You can use ETFs to invest in just about any asset including real estate or even commodities. If you wish to gain exposure to assets such as gold, silver, or oil, you can invest through ETFs.

Commodities are a risky investment and you should be careful before investing your money in them. They move in different cycles compared to the rest of the stock market, which makes it important that you understand how those markets work. Again, you don't have to invest in commodities; you can ignore them and still make money. ETFs make it easy for you to gain broad exposure to different assets and parts of the market with a few simple purchases.

You can buy an ETF that tracks the broad stock market, an ETF that tracks the bond market, and an ETF that tracks the real estate market. With three purchases, you now have a fully diversified and strong portfolio.

Real Estate Investment Trusts

These instruments, also referred to as REITs or "reets" are companies that are heavily invested in real estate. They buy large properties such as residential units, malls, hospitals, parking lots, warehouses, etc. and administer them. They collect rents from their tenants and this forms the profit basis of the REIT.

REITs don't pay corporate taxes thanks to their structure. However, in order to maintain this structure, they need to pay 90% of their profits back to their shareholders as dividends. This means the dividend yield on REITs is quite high. The average REIT yields five to six percent yearly.

Just like with common stocks, investing in individual REITs is risky. These are still companies that can fail. You could buy a REIT that invests in shopping centers and malls. With so many people now moving online, it's possible that the business case for a mall is dead. Another example is a REIT that invests in office buildings.

With companies increasingly embracing remote work, such REITs face an uncertain future. It's far better to therefore invest in an ETF that tracks broadly diversified REITs. This way you earn cash flow through the dividend as well as any capital gains that arise from the rise in the REIT's stock price.

This is an easy and cheap way to invest in real estate. You can invest in just one share of a REIT and earn dividends from your investment. I must mention that if you already own a property and are receiving cash flow from it, you don't need to buy a REIT. The amount of money a property investment requires will give you more than enough exposure to the real estate market.

Other Instruments

There are other instruments you can use to invest your money in such as options, futures, and FX instruments. Truth be told, these aren't investments. They're ways of speculating on short term price movements. They also happen to be needlessly complicated and you don't have to put any money in them in order to make money.

If you do wish to speculate and trade your money then allocate a small portion of your principal, around one percent, and take a trial run. If you manage to make money trading then by all means divert more money into this. You must realize that trading is not a passive activity and you'll have to devote time to it.

The methods of investing I outlined previously are all passive. You don't need to do anything in order to maintain your investment. This will cost you just 0.02% if you invest in the right ETFs. This is a far better method for most people to pursue.

Once you become really wealthy, you'll have access to hedge funds and private equity funds. These pursue complex strategies and charge you a high amount of fees for the privilege of investing in them. If you have over a million dollars to invest, these might appeal to you. Then again, if you had a million you would probably not be reading this book so I'm not going to spend time discussing these.

Real Estate

Real estate is the other major investment of choice for most people. This is understandable since real estate investing is something that people understand better. You can see the property with your own eyes and analyze it a lot better than a stock investment.

There are many ways of making money in real estate and every single one of them involves the use of debt. This means you need to be very careful when running the numbers on a deal. Unless you have enough cash to buy properties outright, you'll have to use financing to have a deal go through.

As I mentioned earlier, as long as there's a mortgage on the property, you do not own it outright. People claiming to own mortgaged property are either clueless or are being deceptive. Successful real estate investors focus on their cash on cash return instead of focusing on the final selling price.

One of the most profitable real estate investment methods is house flipping. Here's how it works. The investor locates a rundown property and buys it using a mortgage. They pay a certain amount of money as a down payment and invest in repairs. This represents their total cash investment.

They then sell the property or earn rent on it. If they sell the property, they get to keep a percentage of the final sales price that represents their ownership in the property. The difference between this amount and the money they invested upfront is their cash on cash return. If they paid less down, and if the repairs boosted the value of the property massively, then their cash on cash return is high.

Here are a few real estate investment strategies that you can utilize:

- House hacking - This is when you live in one of the units in your property and rent out the rest. It's a great starter investment method.
- Turnkey rentals - Buying properties that can be rented immediately or already have tenants in them. This generates instant cash flow.
- Flipping - This is a more advanced strategy since you need to estimate repairs correctly and tailor your offer price appropriately. Financing is also harder to come by since banks won't finance rehabbers.
- Interest only financing - This is the most lucrative yet is the riskiest. This method is described below.

With real estate the terms of financing are extremely important to note. The interest rate and type of loan you receive plays a huge role in determining how the numbers work. You can choose certain types of loans to finance your property investment, but you need to fully understand the risks.

Interest only financing is a case in point. Here's how it works. Let's say you manage to save $100,000. You can buy a property in cash and earn rental returns on it. This will work out to around six to seven percent. You could choose to rehab a property without financing or put it towards rehabbing an expensive property.

You could buy a multi-unit property and earn rentals using traditional financing. Or you could take the riskiest option and purchase a large property with interest only financing with a balloon payment. Such loans have lower monthly payments for a fixed period that then increase dramatically because the principal payments kick in.

The idea is that the investor will sell the property within this time period and make a profit on their cash investment. Profits can be generated by making improvements to the property and by placing it out on rent. If the investor cannot manage the property well or cannot sell the property before the balloon payment (when the monthly payment rises) kicks in, they're in a world of trouble.

It's a high risk and high reward strategy and it brings in astronomical cash on cash returns. It's possible to earn upwards of 50% on such deals. When you consider your cash investment is $100,000, this is a significant return for a few years' work. If it doesn't work out, you're going to be stuck with high principal payments on a property you cannot afford.

I previously gave you an example where a 10% rise in a leveraged investment can bring you a 50% return. This is how it works here as well and all of your real estate investments can be supercharged like this. High leverage deals are not something beginners to real estate should be indulging in. If conditions turn bad and if you cannot exit the deal, you'll bankrupt yourself.

Instead, it's best to invest in house hacking strategies or in turnkey rentals. Make sure the monthly payments are at least one percent of the sale price. If the property is selling for $100,000, make sure the monthly rental is at least $1,000. This will give you a steady cash flow every month and will reduce your mortgage burden as well. You'll build equity in the property steadily over time and increase your net worth.

Tips For Sensible Investment

Here are a few tips you should follow in order to make the best investment possible.

Know Your Risk Profile

Before investing in anything, always consider the worst case scenario and ask yourself how likely it is to happen. For example, if you're going to invest in a diversified broad market ETF, ask yourself how likely it is that this ETF or index will go to zero. If it's remote, you can allocate a larger sum of money towards it.

If you think it's possible that the investment will encounter its worst case scenario, ask yourself how much you're willing to lose on it. If you're saving $2,000 every month, risking $1,000 isn't too much of a risk. You can make this money back in a half a month's time. If the investment can potentially bring you a high return, well above what an ETF can bring, then it's worth investing into.

If you're saving $2,000 per month but are looking at investing $12,000, this is an unintelligent investment. You'll need to work for half a year in order to recover that loss. It just isn't worth it. You can be okay with waiting for a month to recover a potential loss or two months. This depends on your risk profile.

Always ask yourself this question before investing in anything. Don't think of risk as being attached to a particular asset class. I'm mentioning this because you'll often hear people saying that bonds are less risky than stocks and so on. This is untrue. The opportunity defines the risk, not just the instrument.

In many cases, investing in stocks might be less risky than investing in bonds. For example, if a company is going through tough times but is restructuring successfully, it makes sense to buy the stock rather than the bonds. The stock will be selling for a low value while the bonds might likely default if the restructuring falls through.

By buying the stock for a sum that you can afford to lose, you'll capture any potential increase in stock price, which should be substantial, instead of simply earning a fixed rate of interest.

Don't worry if this particular line of reasoning went over your head. You'll understand it once you begin investing your money and this kind of thinking can be learned. My point is to invest in things that match your risk profile. If you're uncertain about something then it's too risky for you, no matter how much of a slam dunk it might be for someone else.

Diversify

If you don't have the time to devote to analyzing the markets in detail, it's best for you to diversify your portfolio. ETF and index fund investing does this for you automatically. As you've already learned, you can gain exposure to a wide variety of asset classes with just three purchases.

The question is how much should you allocate to each asset class? This depends on whether you want cash flow from your investments or capital gains. Capital gains tend to be larger over a period of time but they're riskier to capture. They also happen to be realized as cash only when you sell your investment.

Cash flow from your investments can come in the form of dividends, interest payments from bonds, or rental income. The great thing about cash flow is that you can reinvest it back into your asset and have it generate even more income. With stocks, this is done by opting for a dividend reinvestment program (DRIP).

This automates your investing and you'll earn an increasing amount of cash every year thanks to your ownership increasing. Whichever option you choose, make sure your money is invested in diversified options and isn't concentrated in just a few investments.

If you happen to have the time to actively invest then concentration makes sense. However, make sure you know everything about your investment and aren't investing in something that is outside your sphere of knowledge.

Educate

Investing education never stops. Once you finish reading this book and begin to implement your investing plans, you'll find there are certain nuances that you hadn't thought of previously. You'll return to this book to learn more about these or you'll seek alternative education.

Some things cannot be fully taught. For example, how does one analyze a business? There's no straightforward answer to this. You'll need to go ahead and try to do it and then see what you need to learn. It's an iterative process. You'll need to take action in order to learn more about how investing works.

The same applies to personal finance as well. It's pretty simple to set up a structure that does the job for you. However, fine tuning your personal finance decisions requires education. For example, how much money should you allocate to your side business? What percentage of your monthly income makes sense?

This depends on your own psyche and on your ability to deal with risk. Keep educating yourself on investment options and you'll make progressively better decisions.

Minimize Fees

Fees and taxes will seriously dent your investment returns and you should do your best to minimize them. Brokers don't charge commissions these days so that's a huge positive for you. However, inflation and taxes are ever present. If you invest in funds, you'll have to pay fees for them as well.

Make sure you understand all the fees attached to your investment. Take some time to understand taxes as well since these dent your returns significantly. There are three kinds of taxes you'll pay on your investments:

- Ordinary income.
- Short term capital gains.
- Long term capital gains.

Ordinary income is taxed at the same rate as your regular income. A portion of dividend and interest payments are taxed as ordinary income. Short term capital gains taxes are equal to ordinary income tax levels. These gains are acquired when you sell an asset for a gain within the space of a year.

Long term capital gains are acquired when you sell an asset after holding onto it for more than a year. These tax rates run from zero to 20%. As a result, long term capital gains are taxed at a far lower level than ordinary income or short term capital gains are. This is why investing for the long term makes more money since you'll pay lower taxes.

If you hold onto your asset forever, you'll never pay capital gains taxes since you'll never sell it to realize capital gains. Take the time to understand the tax implications of your investment. For example, physical real estate might cost a lot more than a REIT, but it delivers far more tax benefits than a REIT does.

You can deduct mortgage interest, repairs, and maintenance costs from your tax return. A REIT is a stock holding so you can't do any of this with it. Speak to a tax professional or do your due diligence online to figure out how taxation works.

Start Slow

When you have enough money to invest, you might be tempted to rush ahead and buy everything in sight. However, take the time to understand your choices and invest your money wisely. If you're carrying debt, this is the best time for you to begin educating yourself with regards to how money works.

Study your various options so that when the time comes you'll know exactly what to do with your money. Even if you have a small amount of money to invest, it's important that you put it to work. Leaving your cash lying around is only going to lose you money.

Adopt the mindset that money is meant to work for you and not the other way around. When you're in debt, it will seem as if working for money is the most important thing. However, the way to attain financial freedom is to make money work for you. You do this by preparing and investing it.

Ask for Advice

You don't have to do everything by yourself. Seek advice from financial professionals and books when it comes to figuring out how to invest your money. Understand that not all financial advice is set in stone. Financial advisors often earn money by referring their clients to certain investments.

Seek advice but don't lose your focus on doing what's best for you. No matter how well credentialed someone is, they're not an expert in the market. No one is. After all, no one knows how the markets will perform in the future. The best thing to do is to minimize your risk and invest in the options that allow you to do this. Any good financial advisor will tell you this.

Some people turn to their brokers for investment advice. This is the wrong thing to do. Your broker makes money based on the number of times you trade. The more you trade, the more money they make. Why do you think such an entity will give you good advice? Look for brokers that educate their customers but don't recommend particular investments.

Stick with them as long as they make the risks of investment clear and are upfront about their role. What you want to stay away from are brokers that push certain instruments to you or encourage you to hop in on the latest trends.

Remain as Objective as Possible

There's no denying that money is an emotional topic for everyone. The reason you're reading this book is because you want to earn more money and use it to improve your wellbeing. Once you've invested your money, it can be tough to sit back and see its value decrease.

This happens a lot when people first invest in the stock market. They eagerly track every tick that pushes the value of their investment up or down. This is despite the fact that these gains or losses are unrealized. You won't obtain them unless you sell your investment.

The financial news doesn't do investors any favors either. They constantly broadcast news about some government issue or crisis and elicit either panic or euphoria from their viewers. Every issue is presented as being the biggest thing to ever happen to mankind.

Remember when Brexit was supposed to devastate the economy of the U.K? Before Brexit, Grexit was supposed to decimate the European Union. Before that the housing crisis was supposed to mark the end of Western hegemony in the world. These days, elections and pandemics are supposed to bring about the end of the world.

The media always screams about something or the other. Journalists don't cover the news as much as generate eyeballs for their employers, so it's best to ignore them. The important stuff will find its way to you without any issues. Remain as objective as you can and remember that you're in this for the long term. Don't touch your investments until you're at least 40 years of age. Hold onto them through thick and thin and you'll make money.

Jumping in and out of the market does not make money and you'll end up selling low and buying high. That's the perfect recipe to lose money.

A Final Word

As important as it is to invest in the markets and in instruments that make you money, you need to invest in yourself first and foremost. This is what truly makes you money in the long run. Knowledge has the highest return on investment so allocate money to buy books and learn new skills.

This is why one of the line items in your budget is a self-development contribution. Always invest in yourself and in your health and wellbeing. Whether you make money or not, this investment will always reap rewards for you.

Chapter 7:

Managing Money as a Couple

At some point in the future you might decide to settle down with someone. Perhaps you already have a spouse or partner. Relationships have their own issues and money brings a different dimension of issues with it. Most couples report that money is one of the primary reasons they fight (Slide, 2019).

Much like how we aren't taught to manage our money as individuals, there's no course or class that teaches us how to manage money when we're in a relationship with someone else. Instead, most couples deal with money as if it's the elephant in the room that's being ignored.

This leads to pent up frustrations being voiced when the pressure gets too much and conflict arises. There is a healthy way to deal with money and it begins with acknowledging that it is important for the both of you. You and your partner won't be able to enjoy your life together without money providing things like vacations, entertainment, and essentials like a roof over your heads.

Ignoring money completely is the wrong approach and creates more conflicts. The problem is that as emotional as you get about money, your partner does as well. As bad as we are at dealing with money, we're even worse at handling our emotions in a mature manner.

In this chapter, you're going to learn some of things you can do to reduce the stress that money mismanagement causes in your relationship.

When Should You Talk About it?

The first thing to figure out is when is an appropriate time to begin talking about money? For most couples this occurs when they've been dating for a while and are thinking about either moving in together or are looking to settle down in life with one another.

That's the generic scene that everyone envisions anyway. Reality is a lot more complex than that and has no straightforward answer. So much depends on your personal situation. What if you dated someone for six months and then discovered your partner has $70,000 in student loan debt? If they happened to be working a steady job and had plans to pay it off, you might be willing to stay with them.

But what if this was credit card debt? Won't debt of this size indicate an uncontrolled spending pattern? Everyone wants to marry for love but practical considerations often overshadow things. When it comes to money, you're hitching your credit and future to someone else's.

Understand that when you get married, you become legally liable for your spouse's debt. This varies depending on the state in which the debt was incurred, but it goes to show that entering into a long term relationship with someone is no joke. This is why the standard thought process of waiting for six months to a year before approaching the topic of money doesn't work for some people.

You can't control the other person's behavior but you sure can control your own. If your financial situation happens to be precarious, you owe it to the other person to let them know about it. Being honest upfront is the best way to prevent any future drama. If you have student loan debt and are working hard at paying it off and reducing your debt burden, letting them know how you're going about doing this is a practical thing to do.

More importantly, by doing this you'll automatically attract people who are also aware of how their money is being spent. While you're dealing with financial problems of your own, you don't want to find out your partner has greater financial issues than yours a year into the relationship.

If your situation happens to be perfectly fine, it's still okay to mention this and talk about it. The intention isn't to brag or to show off how smart you are. It's just being genuine. What are your views on mortgages and how do you think they should be dealt with? It's not the most romantic of topics to discuss, but what do you lose by spending a ew minutes discussing this?

It's just common sense to do this. Too many people buy into the script of romance sustaining everything in a relationship and this might be true. However, it's so much easier to romance someone who is conscious of their financial position and is working hard to rectify any holes in it.

So make it a point to talk about it upfront. You don't need to know or ask how much someone makes from their job or business. That just makes you look like a gold digger and makes people uncomfortable. However, you do have a right to know of any red flags with regards to debt. Understand that if you're talking about money for the first time when you're deciding to move in together, it's already too late.

It's not a problem if neither of you have any serious financial concerns. However, if there are concerns it will put significant strain on your relationship. You've already invested time into it and having money interfere with it will raise feelings of guilt. It might feel awkward to talk about it early on but do it. If you do end up in a relationship with that person, at least you'll know that money isn't going to become a barrier between the two of you.

Blueprints

You'll learn more about this in the next chapter but all of us have a certain blueprint surrounding money within us. This blueprint is just the sum of our beliefs about money and about how it ought to be used. We develop these when we're young and impressionable.

Most of our beliefs solidify before the age of five. The scary part is that we're barely conscious at this point. We're completely dependent on our parents at that age and simply absorb everything they tell us. We learn how to behave by watching what they do. As a result, we grow up with all these beliefs in our minds about money that dictate what our financial life will look like.

The good news is that these blueprints can be unlearned. You can install new beliefs in your mind. I'll talk about the right beliefs in the next chapter. For now, let's focus on asking the right kinds of questions of your partner so that you can get an idea of how they view money.

It isn't just their financial situation you want to understand but also how they believe money ought to be used. This will help you understand their spending patterns and habits in the future. Let's say the two of you decide that saving money is a priority but then your partner goes and buys a new blender.

This might strike you as being unnecessary but according to them, it might be extremely necessary since they cannot do without its assistance when cooking food. Who's to say who's right or wrong in this situation? A lot of couples find themselves in situations like this and don't deal with it well. If they had sat down and asked themselves the following questions, such situations could have potentially been prevented.

- Life goals - What is your partner's biggest goal in life and are they working towards it? This is a pretty weighty question to ask, but it lets you know whether they have an established direction in their life. You can't expect someone to divulge this immediately upon meeting them, but it's an appropriate question to ask at some point once you become close.

- How should couples manage money? Ask them what their thoughts are on how couples ought to split finances and manage money. Some couples combine everything, some split it completely, and some adopt a hybrid method. Get their thoughts on this and turn it into a discussion. You'll learn more about them in the process.

- How do they feel about saving and investing together? Ask them if they think joint investing goals are something to aspire to or if people are better off investing separately. In some cases where the investment is shared it makes sense. However, what if the investing activities of one person disrupts that of the other? There is no right answer to these questions. The aim is to get a feel for how well you gel together and how honest they are with you.

- Which budget considerations are you the most sensitive about? You might be willing to reduce your entertainment expenses to save more but are they willing to do this? What if they cannot do without organic food (expensive) but you're perfectly fine with eating ramen (super cheap) all day? Aside from diet questions, this is a topic that most couples clash about since one person's spending might not make sense to the other. So talk it out.

- How did your family manage money? Figuring out what their childhood financial environment was like will help you understand a lot about their spending habits. You might find that your partner makes a lot of money but still insists on buying clothes when they're on sale. They might be extremely conservative with their investments and might be incurring opportunity costs they can't see. This is pretty typical of someone who grew up in low income households since they cannot look beyond cash on hand and the concept of opportunity costs is rarely discussed.
- Do you have a retirement plan? What is retirement to you? These questions are self-explanatory. You want someone who has a basic plan in place. They don't need to have all the answers, but some direction with regards to their future direction is important.
- How do you see your income evolving in the long run? The answer to this question will tell you how they view side hustles and side businesses. Someone who has just one source of income is one step away from poverty in today's world. Never forget that. With automation and disruption on the rise, your job might be taken by a robot in the near future. Companies do not owe you anything and they know it. If you have a plan in place to develop a second source of income, you want someone who's on the same page regarding that.

How you ask these questions is pretty important. Asking them directly as I've listed them above might put your partner on the defensive and give off the wrong vibes. You want to broach the topic in a sensitive manner and make it clear that the point of these questions isn't to judge them.

You might find that your partner is not on the same wavelength as you with regards to these topics. However, do they see the sense in your point of view? Or do they dismiss it completely as being irrelevant and insist that they are right? It's pretty obvious how such a relationship will turn out.

How you choose to take the relationship forward is up to you, but at the very least your partner should be willing to communicate with you on the topic of money and finances. If they constantly become insecure when talking about it, you're entering a world of conflict down the road.

Money Management Tips

Aside from the tips provided in the previous section, you'll do well to follow the directions here when it comes to money management as part of a relationship.

Discuss Prenuptial or Postnuptial Agreements

Most couples decide to talk about this only when they're about to get married and it has the potential to derail everything they've built together. Instead of leaving it to the last moment, discuss the topic well in advance. You don't have to talk about it with regards to the two of you.

Get their thoughts on the topic in general. What do they think about this and how do they view it? A common argument is that such agreements decrease the romance in a relationship and throw cold water on things. The truth is that such agreements protect both parties and it's in both of your best interests to discuss it.

If one partner has significantly more assets than the other, it's essential for the couple to have some sort of nuptial agreement either before the marriage or after it. Again, I'm not saying you need to propose marriage through the discussion of this topic. Your goal should be to gather their thoughts on the subject.

Other conditions that necessitate a nuptial agreement is if one party inherits a large sum of money, if one of you has a successful business, or if one party has familial wealth far in excess of the other. Such agreements only strengthen the bond between the two of you since you're being completely honest about each other's financial situations.

If your partner happens to have children from another marriage or relationship, this necessitates a nuptial agreement as well since there are multiple claims on their assets. Start talking about this topic well before you ever reach the altar. The sooner you begin talking about this and clear any issues, the better your relationship will be.

Be Honest

This one goes without saying but it's pretty tough to do. The last thing you want to do is embarrass yourself in front of a person you like. However, you should be honest about your financial situation if there are any red flags in it. As I said earlier, you owe it to your partner to let them know of any situation.

Thinking that you'll suddenly come clean one fine day after you've been together for a while is a childish way of handling things. It's a lot easier to kick the can down the road, but it just compounds your problems. You want to compound your money instead of your issues.

If your financial situation is fine, you can still broach the topic of debt and ask them for their views on it. At the very least you'll have an interesting conversation with them about what they would do if they found out their partner has a ton of debt. It's something to bond over, as unromantic as it sounds.

Develop Goals

While individual financial goals are important, you should take the time to develop shared goals as well. You're going to be sharing your lives and assets together if things go well, so this only makes sense. One of the most common goals is to own a home together.

There are many questions you'll need to consider when figuring out this goal. How much will each of you contribute towards it? Will these contributions determine who gets more equity in the property? How else will you determine that? Will you need a separate agreement over this?

Discuss these issues in detail and figure out how you'll deal with them. Another goal could be to get rid of debt together even if one person is carrying the debt load. For example, you could be carrying student loan debt but your partner might be debt free. How will they help you get rid of this load?

Will they contribute to it or help you financially in some way? If you're going to be getting rid of debt, you'll need to sacrifice certain things in your life. How will they cope with this? You might not be able to afford a fancy night out and will have to figure out how to keep them satisfied without spending too much money.

Talk all of these issues out together. Another important thing to discuss is your list of individual goals. You might have a roomful of goals but your partner might not have any. How will you help them figure out what their goals need to be? Do they even need goals if they're doing just fine without them?

Bank Accounts

Once the goal discussion is done, you'll need to move onto the practical aspects of money management and discuss how you'll handle the issue of bank accounts. Most couples have a hybrid system where they have a single joint account from which both parties pay for shared expenses.

In this method both parties have individual bank accounts where they maintain how much ever balance suits them. The joint account is used to pay for shared living expenses such as housing and groceries. You can even choose to maintain your six month living expenses balance in this account along with any other emergency funds.

Typically this account will have a single credit card attached to it and all living expenses are passed through it. Given that both people will have access to the card and its spending limit, it's crucial to talk about who gets to keep the card and what sort of limits need to be maintained.

A common problem under this system is that sometimes spending gets mixed up. For example, one person needs to buy clothes for themselves and this isn't a shared expense. However, it gets clubbed together with shared expenses due to everything being paid for at once.

It's important to schedule a time for the two of you to review your expenses and categorize them accordingly. This is the same exercise that you do with your own budget; you're just doing it together. Over time, you might find it's easier for just one of you to do it, but it's always helpful for the two of you to engage with this.

Investment accounts also need to be discussed thoroughly. If the two of you have separate accounts, combining them might make sense. This is especially the case if you wish to file as a couple. You'll earn tax benefits by doing this since the limits for tax brackets are higher. You'll also earn the ability to claim larger deductions.

You cannot hold a retirement account jointly. However, a spousal IRA does exist wherein one spouse contributes a sum to the other's IRA if the primary account holder cannot contribute too much. It might be worth discussing this option if your desire is to provide some sort of a safety net for your partner.

There are other accounts that need to be discussed as well. For instance, how will life insurance be handled? Life insurance claims have often been at the center of murder plots in Hollywood movies so they've earned an undeserved reputation. However, a large life insurance policy held by one partner has the potential to skew things in the relationship.

You need to discuss this in detail and be open in your communication throughout. There is no boilerplate method to get through this. You'll just have to trust your instincts and judge the situation as best as you can.

Share Tasks

You should view budgeting and tracking expenses as an extension of your household chores. Sometimes the partner that feels uncomfortable with money lets the other take care of everything. This is not optimal. Just because one partner feels they cannot be good with money doesn't mean they can absolve themselves of that task.

The reason is that this puts undue pressure on the other person, even if they enjoy handling money and budgeting. At the end of the day, you're a partnership and you need to share some burden of the tasks. At the very least, the person who doesn't enjoy the task should know the high level situation with regards to money.

You can also divide the tracking tasks between yourselves to ease the burden from one partner's plate. This will help the other person realize that their belief about them being bad with money is just an illusion and that anyone can learn to get good with it.

Plan to Attack Debt

It's quite common these days for both partners to be carrying some level of debt with them. Whether it's student loan debt, car payments, credit card debt, you need to work to eliminate it. If you're carrying a mortgage without generating cash flow, you need to work at developing cash flow right now.

In case the mortgage as debt argument hasn't sunk in yet, here's a simple explanation. When you buy an asset you earn money from it in two ways. Either through appreciation in its price or through cash flow. When you purchase a stock, you're earning income in both ways even if it doesn't pay a dividend. Why is this?

Well, a stock represents a business and businesses earn money and revenues. You might not be getting paid but those revenues fuel stock price increases. Thus, you're earning both cash flow and capital gains through that cash flow. This is why investing solely in dividends isn't the only way to invest successfully in stocks.

However, a traditional residential property isn't a place of business. People live in it. It's value does not increase just because you're earning rent from it. They're two separate streams of income. If you live in it without generating cash flow, you're only earning half of the possible income streams. Even then capital gains are unrealized and you will not see this money until you sell the place.

Cash flow is something you can use right now. It reduces debt burden and you can pay your mortgage and maintain the property with it. In some areas, especially near universities, you can earn a greater amount of cash through rents than your mortgage payment. In essence you'll get paid to own the property.

Coming back to your activities as a couple, you need to attack debt. Check to see if there's a way you can consolidate your debt as a couple. This isn't always possible or practical if one partner doesn't have debt, but it's worth a shot. Once the debt is consolidated, you can work together to develop a plan to eliminate it.

This means you'll need to go through the goal definition exercise together and develop a plan of action. This should be exciting since the two of you are plotting your way towards financial freedom. Make sure to keep tabs on your goals and once you get there, you'll find it extra special.

Handling Arguments and Disagreements

Conflict is inevitable. This doesn't mean you need to scream and shout at one another, as tempting as that might sound. As I mentioned earlier, finances are the most common thing that couples argue about. In fact, they're the most common reason for divorce. Open communication from the beginning will ensure that most problems will be averted.

However, it's not possible to account for all problems. Here are some tips to help you deal with conflict in an amicable way.

Empathize

Remember when you learned about blueprints? One of the reasons you and your partner clash with one another is due to your blueprints conflicting. Getting to know your own blueprint is just as important as understanding your partner's. The best way to understand their point of view is to put yourself in their shoes.

It's not easy to do this in the heat of the moment so take some time to step away if things get heated. It might help to have an argument handling protocol as well. No one wins when all you do is scream at one another. Taking some time away from each other to cool down will help you empathize with your partner and lead to better solutions to your problem.

Enforce Boundaries

Discipline is hard to enforce when you're trying to apply it to yourself. Doing it as a couple is tougher. However, it's far from impossible. As long as your goals are clearly communicated and you understand each other's money blueprints, striking to your chosen path should be straightforward, even if it is challenging.

One of the keys to enforcing discipline is to set boundaries when it comes to communication. In terms of spending, what kind of behavior is acceptable and how will you communicate your issues with one another? Talking these things out in advance is extremely helpful and will prevent further issues down the road.

Take responsibility for your actions and communicate the importance of this to your partner. Keep an open mind as much as possible and don't assume your partner can read your thoughts.

Compromise

Successful relationships are all about how well you compromise with one another. It's no different when it comes to spending habits. This is why the hybrid system of managing money through three bank accounts (at a minimum) works really well. It gives both people the space to indulge in the things they want without compromising the wellbeing of the relationship.

Of course, not every problem has such an elegant solution. There will be times when you'll need to compromise and give in on the point you're arguing. Giving in all the time means you aren't compromising. You're not setting strong enough boundaries.

It's best to talk about these issues as soon as they occur to avoid stewing over them. Such issues usually burst out at the worst possible moment and communication breaks down even further.

When arguing your point, it's important to maintain a steady state and not get agitated. Getting angry or frustrated only makes things worse. It helps to have a rule that neither of you will go to bed agitated or angry. It's not necessary to hash everything out immediately, but try to at least agree to discuss things right away when you wake up.

Talk About Money

Most people are uncomfortable talking about money. If this applies to you, it isn't your fault. This is how society and our education system lets us down when it comes to financial education. There's a lot of awkwardness surrounding money. Even in sectors such as finance, it's taboo to talk about money as it relates to someone personally.

Whatever the world might think about money, you owe it to yourself and your partner to review your finances and money situation. Talk about your money as often as it makes sense and don't ignore it. This only makes it even more difficult to get a handle on your finances.

Setup a schedule where you and your partner review your financial status every week. Even if this lasts for just 15 minutes, it's worth it. This is especially the case if one of you happens to think they're bad with money or cannot figure out numbers.

Seek Help

If things get out of control and if you find that no amount of talking or communication seems to be alleviating your financial problems, you should seek professional help. Talk to a debt management professional or a financial advisor who will be able to guide you on the finer points of handling your finances.

Chapter 8:

The Psychology of Wealth

Being wealthy and having financial independence are worthy goals to aim for. However most people make the mistake of thinking of these things as being all about money. While money is central to them, the fact is that your psyche and your mindset surrounding money is what brings these results.

I mentioned previously how lottery winners are more likely to file for bankruptcy within three years of winning when compared to the average American. Their minds are simply unable to cope with their new found prosperity, which results in a series of bad decisions that chases money away.

Getting wealthy seems hard due to the barriers your own mind has been placing in front of you. Making money is actually quite straightforward. What's tricky is convincing your mind that you deserve this money and that it truly belongs to you. You've grown up with harmful beliefs surrounding money.

I can say this with a high degree of confidence because you're reading this book looking for solutions that will make your personal financial life a bit easier. This is a great step you've taken. Now it's time to dig a little deeper and ask yourself what these beliefs are.

You don't need to conduct a Freudian psychoanalysis on yourself. Instead, recall the statements you heard about money when growing up. What was your environment like? Were your parents good with money or did they mismanage it? Your parents might have been good with money, but perhaps they held certain beliefs that go against the notion of abundance.

This is often the case with people who manage to save money. They hang onto it as if they'll never receive money again. As a result, when they try to go out and make some, money deserts them because they believe it to be scarce or too hard to make. Perhaps this is what has been going on with you.

Did your parents believe something negative about rich people? Did they tell you that money doesn't grow on trees, that the stock market was rigged, or that rich people were immoral or evil? All of these beliefs exert themselves in unconscious ways in your life. You've been practicing them without knowing they even exit.

The way to repair your money blueprint and rectify these beliefs is to simply follow new habits. This is easier said than done. Your old habits will pull you back towards them since your brain loves being comfortable. However, make it a point to practice these habits and apply your utmost awareness to what you're saying and doing. Awareness alone will help you unravel these unhelpful thoughts and you'll find yourself changing the way you look at money.

The Wealth Mindset

Constructing a mindset of wealth is as simple as practicing the right habits. Before you begin practicing these habits it's important for you to do two things. First, you need to recognize that your existing beliefs aren't your own. They've been passed down to you by your parents and caregivers from a young age.

You were forced to learn them because you simply didn't know any better. This isn't your parents' fault or anyone else's. In fact, now that you've become aware of their existence, you can take steps to change your learned beliefs.

The second thing to do is to fix an intention in your mind. Intentionality is extremely powerful since it helps your brain focus better. You might have problems with this initially, but your brain will soon learn and help you. Fixing an intention is as simple as telling yourself that you want to build a wealthy mindset. Tell yourself this with everything you do.

Tell yourself this when you wake up in the morning and before you go to bed. When you're out shopping, tell yourself you want to build and are building a wealthy mindset. Your mind will automatically begin searching for information that pertains to this intention. You'll be exposed to solutions and other resources that will help you.

You'll still need to do the work. You'll have to execute certain habits that wealthy people possess. These habits are automatic for them and this is why they have all the money they need.

Think for the Long Term

The most important thing you can do is to think and plan for the long term. This applies to everything from the way you plan your budget to the way you track your spending. It also clarifies the need versus want question. In the moment, it can be challenging to decide which category a particular purchase falls into.

Spending money with a view to building long term wealth will also help you build patience. A large fortune is not built in a day. There's a reason the average 65 year old has more wealth than the average 22 year old. It takes time to earn and amass money.

Money also takes some time to get going and bring you results. We're not talking about months or years but decades here. This is why it's important for you to start investing as soon as possible so that you give your money the longest runway possible.

Build strategies to control your short term cravings. Instead of trying to eliminate them completely, it's best to allocate a small amount of money to them. There's no reason for you to be unkind to yourself. Much like how dieters allocate one meal per week to eat whatever they desire, no matter how unhealthy, you can allocate a small amount of money towards buying these wants.

Over time, you'll find that the pleasure these one off purchases bring will decrease and you'll automatically divert that money towards long term spending. What are some examples of expenses that are beneficial for the long term? Here's a small list:

- Side hustle or side business fund contributions.
- Courses and skill upgrades.
- Personal development and learning through books.
- Taking care of your health by investing in a gym membership or health classes.
- Health and life insurance.
- Retirement plan contributions.
- Buying the best food you can afford.
- Buying good clothes and shoes that last for a long time as opposed to chasing brand names every other month.
- Spending money on market research for your proposed business.

Read and Learn

The wealthiest people in the world all have one thing in common: they read. Bill Gates reads close to 52 books every year. That's one book every week. Over the course of a year, he manages to compound his knowledge to such an extent that the average person cannot hope to keep up with him.

Gates is rich enough to be retired and pursue the things that are the most important to him. You might think you don't have such luxuries. However, examine your day and you'll find that there are many opportunities for you to speed up your learning.

What do you do when you eat lunch or other meals? Do you stare into your phone for mindless entertainment? Every once in a while such a release is necessary, but do you need to do it every single time?

Here's a simple experiment you can conduct: Sell your TV and cancel your cable or streaming subscriptions. Leave yourself with no easy access to entertainment. You'll find yourself automatically reading books. If you struggle reading books and cannot remain focused, read them in small batches. Read just 10 pages everyday. If you use an electronic reader, read a fixed percentage of the book, say five percent.

The average book sold on the market contains around 300 pages. If you read 10 pages everyday, you'll get through a book in a month. That's far from Gates' average but he does have the luxury of doing whatever he wants. Having said that, 12 books a year is nothing to sniff at.

What kind of books should you read? Preferably, something that challenges your thinking. Paperback fiction is highly entertaining and you'll get through these books in no time, but they don't add much to your life. However, there's no harm in reading these books once in a while.

Aim to read at least 10 books that challenge your views of the world or enhance them. If you can't afford books for whatever reason, read blogs and articles on the internet surrounding your chosen topics. You can also view videos on YouTube about topics you're curious about.

Spend Money to Make Money

A big difference between the rich and not so rich is that the former spend money building assets. Your biggest asset is your brain and the skills it helps you execute. The not so rich want everything for free because they think they don't have enough money to spend on assets.

This is true in many ways. The reason people become less than rich is because they spend far too much on entertainment and distraction. The rich focus on spending money on things that add to their lives, not distract them from it. I'm not saying you should not entertain yourself. It's just that your definition of entertainment needs to be changed.

Here's something you can do right away. Do you spend money buying yourself a cup of coffee everyday? Instead of buying one and drinking it by yourself, invite someone you admire and buy them a cup of coffee. Tell them in advance that you'd like to ask them some questions about how they handle things and would love to buy them a coffee to discuss it.

This is powerful in so many ways. First, you're demonstrating to the other person that you have an abundance mindset. Knowledge grows when it is shared and this is something every truly wealthy person knows. Second, you're developing your own skills and mindset by associating with the other person and are growing. Third, and this is the best one, you've turned your daily coffee into an asset where it was previously a liability!

If you're thinking that this method will now result in you spending double on coffee everyday, then your mind is not in tune with the abundance mindset. If increasing your coffee spending is not possible, then why not buy something cheaper for yourself instead of a coffee? There's no rule that says you need to drink coffee with the other person despite buying them one.

This applies to almost everything you do. In order to start a business, you need to spend money testing the market and your product. You need to spend money advertising. You potentially need to spend money hiring employees. You need to spend money increasing your skills via education.

Spending money to build an asset is very different from spending it on a liability. Here's a simple question the wealthy ask themselves before spending money: What is the long term value I can receive from this expense? What is the value of the things this expense will bring me and how long will this value last?

Persistence

Thinking long term is the underlying theme of the wealth mindset. This means you need to work hard until you're exhausted and then work some more. Everyone imagines sandy beaches and sipping cocktails with little straw hats on them, but this takes time to build.

The good news is it takes less time than you might think. The key is to be consistent with your work and show up over and over again. Take care to avoid the mindless work trap. This happens when people target a certain number of hours to work every week or day.

Your mind doesn't work like this. There are some days when you need to allow it to relax and do nothing. Listen to your body and mind. They know what's best for you. Don't look at your efforts as something you need to do over a single day. Instead, treat it as something you need to do for at least a year or two. Focus on execution and let everything else fade away.

Work Smart

The "number of hours worked" trap can be avoided by working smart. What does working smart mean though? It begins by setting an intention upfront. Before you sit down to work, what is your objective? This will help you minimize distraction.

When you begin working, eliminate as many distractions as possible. Preferably you won't need the internet, but these days that's a bit far fetched. Instead, set up website blockers, turn off your phone, and restrict all notifications. Focus on the job at hand and on executing your intention.

Now do this over and over for as long as you're mentally able to do it. Sometimes your mind will need a breather to process the information it has learned. You might find yourself unable to focus for a few days. This is fine. Listen to your mind and once it's done processing information, you'll find that you've leveled up in terms of knowledge.

Consistency is the key to smart work. Results are not created through a single work session. They're the product of repeated and focused work. Don't compare the number of hours you work to someone else. Instead, compare the quality of your work sessions to your previous sessions. This is how progress is achieved.

Keep Good Company

You are the product of those you hangout and identify with. Who are the five people you interact with on an almost daily basis? That's who you are. This isn't rocket science. If you want to be as rich as Jeff Bezos, you need to hang out with him. Unfortunately, Bezos is less than accessible to you right now.

This isn't a problem though. Your mind doesn't know the difference between physically associating with someone and mentally associating with them. In fact, your brain cannot even tell the difference between a real experience and an imagined one. This is why visualization is so powerful.

Consume as much content as you can that is associated with the people you wish to identify with. Think about what they're saying and ask them questions in your mind. In his famous book *Think and Grow Rich* Napoleon Hill described a method wherein he held nightly conversations with the people he admired the most.

He described holding round table conversations with Abraham Lincoln, Theodore Roosevelt, Henry Ford, and Thomas Edison. He even gave them personality quirks and conducted meetings with them. You can do the same thing. These days you can consume content much more easily than in Hill's days thanks to YouTube videos.

If you want to invest like Buffett, then search for the annual meetings of his company where he and Charlie Munger answer questions from investors. Associate with the way these people think and you'll create massive changes in your own life. Who knows, you might even end up meeting some of them in person in an informal setting.

Seek a Mentor

Mentorship is a powerful way to boost your success. I'm not talking about the fake mentorship that internet frauds sell you. A true mentor doesn't want to be paid. This person is someone who has achieved what you want and whose results you'd like to replicate.

The key difference between a mentor and the tactic I described previously is that a mentor is physically accessible to you. So how do you find such a person? It's easier than you think. Look around you and see who you admire. They might not have the level of success you desire, but there might be something else you admire about them.

Perhaps they conduct themselves a certain way or perhaps they have professional skills you greatly admire. Use the coffee tactic to start talking to them. You don't need to tell them you're seeking mentoring. However, if someone takes a liking to you, you'll find that they'll share their knowledge with you willingly.

If you're looking to switch jobs and admire a personality or a high level executive in your field, reach out to them for an informational interview. This is a tactic you can use if you're in college and you'll put yourself miles ahead of other applicants for a job.

Instead of asking to be interviewed (which is how job searches work), interview your prospective boss and ask them all about what they do and how their industry works. Ask them questions about their mindset and how they handle problems. This form of sincere appreciation will leave a mark and you'll find them more receptive to your questions.

In short, whether they know it or not, they'll mentor you.

Expand

Successful people are always seeking to expand their comfort zone. They understand that seeking to remain in the same spot is the best way to go backwards. Look at the habits of the average unsuccessful or unhappy person and you'll see that they do their best to remain stationary or static. They're not comfortable entertaining the idea of change and cling onto the past. They reminisce about the old days or wish for a time when things will be easy.

In contrast, happy people are content with the present and are appreciative of everything they have. This doesn't mean they're stagnant or that they're not looking to grow. In fact, they're looking to add to their roll of assets. Over time, money comes to them easily because they're up to speed with the changes taking place around them and are providing value to people.

Money is made when you provide utility or value. It isn't donated to you. In order to determine what people value, you need to push your comfort zone and remain up to speed with your field.

Understand Risk

Unsuccessful people do not understand risk. The best person to talk to about risk and the mindset associated with risk is a businessperson. These people handle risk everyday and understand that risk is just half the equation. The other half is reward.

As long as you can cover your downside risk and if the reward is worth it, you should go ahead and assume the risk. For example, if you can buy an Instagram account for $3,000 and monetize it to the tune of $1,000 per month, this is a great opportunity. The risk here is that you cannot monetize it at all and your $3,000 goes to waste.

If you have just $3,000 in your bank account, this is a huge risk. You're placing your entire business capital on the block. If you have $10,000 in business capital, you can stomach this better. Risk assessment isn't just about capital size though. If you have $3,000 in capital but if you can raise this money through savings in a month or two months, it's worth the risk.

After all, you're losing just two months' worth of capital. If you've spent a year saving this much then you need to ask yourself whether you're willing to spend an entire year rebuilding this amount. This is where reward assessment comes into play. If the investment brings you $12,000 in revenues per year, is it worth risking a year's savings of $3,000?

Some people might not be okay with this. Some might be. Ask yourself these questions to figure out what your risk to reward ratio is like and act accordingly.

Eliminate Scarcity Thinking

You have much more going for you than you're aware of. What were the odds of you even being born? Are you alive? Are you healthy? Do you have access to food and clean water? Congratulations, you're in the top 10 percent of people around the world.

No matter how small a positive is, celebrate it. This isn't about denying the negatives in your life. Instead, acknowledge they exist but also recognize that there are things that are very right with your life. Scarcity attracts more scarcity while abundance does the same.

Abundant thinking isn't about jumping around for joy at every little thing. Instead, it's maintaining a balanced perspective and believing that you'll figure things out. It's recognizing that even in the worst situations, there are things that are positive and that not everything is negative.

It's about focusing on the existence of something as opposed to the lack of it. You don't get money by thinking of how little of it exists in your life. You get it by focusing on how to generate more of it, even if it's just a single cent every month. Celebrate that cent. It's a positive and deserves to be celebrated!

Conclusion

Personal finance is one of the most important topics that you'll learn about in your life. It's truly tragic that our education system has been letting us down for so long. However, there's nothing to be done about this. Instead, you should focus on educating yourself in the things that are essential to you.

Improving your financial situation is all about doing two things: lowering your expenses and making more money. Before you try to make more money, you need to take an inventory of your expenses and figure out which ones you can reduce or turn into an asset.

For example, you could drive for Uber and reduce your car expenditure. You could sell your clothes on eBay or donate them and claim a tax deduction. You can practice minimalism in your life and thereby reduce the number of possessions you need to worry about.

Create a budget and track your expenses properly. You've already learned about the habits you need to adopt to do this successfully. Focus on executing these habits and don't worry too much about how things will turn out. Live in the moment and avoid time traveling between the future and the past.

Making money is as simple as providing value. The internet has ensured that you can provide value far more easily these days than in the past. You've read about a number of side hustles and businesses you can begin with very little investment. Work towards establishing a second source of income and your wealth will start working for you.

Above all else you need to eliminate debt. Treat it as your mortal enemy because of the harm it causes your financial life.

You're one step closer to being financially free now. Keep building on the momentum you've generated and follow the steps in this book. Go out there and use these tools and watch as your life and wealth grow.

If you have enjoyed the material in the book, please consider leaving an honest review online. Thank you for purchasing my book. Stay safe and enjoy your day!

I wish you all the luck in the world!

References

Carter, M. (2019, March 15). What Is the Average Time to Repay Student Loans? *Credible*. https://www.credible.com/blog/statistics/average-time-to-repay-student-loans-statistics/

El Issa, E., & O'Shea, B. (2020, March 17). *Why Did My Credit Score Drop After Paying Off Debt?* NerdWallet. https://www.nerdwallet.com/article/finance/credit-score-drop-pay-debt

Godfrey, N. (2020, January 4). *Day Trading: Smart Or Stupid?* Forbes. https://www.forbes.com/sites/nealegodfrey/2017/07/16/day-trading-smart-or-stupid/#7401df691007

Haynes, T. (2018, April 30). Dopamine, Smartphones, & You: A battle for your time. *SITNBoston*. http://sitn.hms.harvard.edu/flash/2018/dopamine-smartphones-battle-time/

Hess, A. (2017, August 25). *Here's why lottery winners go broke*. CNBC. https://www.cnbc.com/2017/08/25/heres-why-lottery-winners-go-broke.html

Hess, A. (2019, May 20). *Here's how much the average student loan borrower owes when they graduate*. CNBC. https://www.cnbc.com/2019/05/20/how-much-the-average-student-loan-borrower-owes-when-they-graduate.html

Martin, E. (2017, November 20). *Here's how much money you need to be happy, according to a new analysis by wealth experts*. CNBC. https://www.cnbc.com/2017/11/20/how-much-money-you-need-to-be-happy-according-to-wealth-experts.html

Slide, C. (2019, August 5). *18 Money Management Tips for Newly Married Couples.* Moneycrashers.Com. https://www.moneycrashers.com/money-management-newly-married-couples/

All images retrieved from www.pixabay.com

Printed in Great Britain
by Amazon

21313007R00099